christmas cookies

from the

WHIMSICAL BAKEHOUSE

christmas cookies

from the

WHIMSICAL BAKEHOUSE

kaye hansen & liv hansen

PHOTOGRAPHS BY BEN FINK

CLARKSON POTTER/PUBLISHERS

NEW YORK

Printed in Singapore

Design by Jan Derevjanik

Library of Congress Cataloging-in-Publication Data
Hansen, Kaye
    Christmas cookies from the whimsical bakehouse /
Kaye Hansen and Liv Hansen.
    Includes index.
1. Cookies   2. Christmas cookery.   I. Hansen, Liv.
II. Title.
TX772.H37   2005
641.8'654—dc22   2004022026

ISBN 1-4000-8058-4

10   9   8   7   6   5   4   3   2   1

First Edition

acknowledgments

First and foremost we want to thank everyone who enjoyed our first book, *The Whimsical Bakehouse: Fun-to-Make Cakes That Taste as Good as They Look.* We appreciate all of your wonderful feedback and support. We hope you continue to be inspired by these recipes and decorations. We also want to acknowledge the efforts of everyone at the Bakehouse, including Lavar Daisy, Marianna Cintron, and Karen Marconi; we know what a sacrifice sampling and resampling our cookies was! Special thanks to our friends in Canada: Pam, Meagan, and Katherine Heus. Thank you for home testing our recipes, even though confectioners' sugar is difficult to find way up north. Our sincerest thanks to: Adina Steiman for taking another chance with us and guiding us through the process one more time; Carla Glasser for being our tireless advocate; and Ben Fink, who once again helped bring our vision to vivid life.

contents

introduction

YES, IT'S THAT TIME OF YEAR AGAIN. SHIMMERING lights, jubilant decorations wherever your eyes roam, and, of course, scrumptious cookies. Christmas just wouldn't be the same without an assortment of festive cookies, from simple butter cookies to whimsical gingerbread houses. These are truly *Christmas* cookies, inspired by the first snow, roaring fireplaces, the spicy scent of cinnamon, and steamy mugs of hot cocoa. Just a glance at a plate of dazzling Christmas cookies, decorated in rich reds and greens and icy palettes of blue and glistening white, and you and your loved ones will instantly get in the holiday mood.

Cookies are always a popular item at the Bakehouse, but at Christmas we can't make enough of them. My mom is always coming up with new cookie recipes, and I'm always imagining new ways to decorate them. Our Nutty Thumbprint Cookies and Walnut Acorns have been a Christmas tradition ever since I was a toddler. But each Christmas I find a new favorite, like the latest addition to our repertoire: Shortbread Snowflakes. Most of these recipes follow the advice my grandmother passed on to my mom—that cookies made with confectioners' sugar are the most tender. Years of baking has taught my mom that this is true. She also believes that anything baked with butter is better, and is notorious for changing recipes to suit this fancy, replacing oil or shortening with good old-fashioned butter. So as you'll see, very few recipes in this book lack that special ingredient, making every cookie more scrumptious, rich, and irresistible.

This book is composed of seven sections: "Getting Started," "Hand-Formed Cookies," "Seasonal Sliced Cookies," "Piped Cookies," "Bar Cookies," "Christmas Cutout Cookies," and "Fancy Decorated Cookies." For best results, we suggest you begin with "Getting Started." This section contains numerous helpful hints and tips from both of us based on lessons we've learned through generations of cookie baking. In addition, we have included essential information on useful baking and decorating tools employed often throughout the book.

Christmas is a very hectic time of year—a time when people who usually don't bake find themselves in the kitchen trying out new recipes. If you are new to baking, start with a recipe marked "easy" ( ), because these cookies are not only simple to make, but also simple to decorate. Most of the recipes found in the "Hand-Formed Cookies" and the "Seasonal Sliced Cookies" chapters are considered easy. Just remember to read through the recipes from start to finish before beginning, and make sure you have all of the necessary ingredients. Some of the more challenging recipes (marked "medium" 🌲🌲 or "difficult" 🌲🌲🌲) might take more time. Still, even these more elaborate cookies are do-able and they are definitely worth the extra effort.

If you expect a hectic Christmas (and who doesn't?), it's helpful to know that most of our cookies freeze beautifully, and many of the unbaked doughs can also be frozen for future baking.

As much as Christmas is a season of food and family, it is also a season of wondrous décor and festive sights: Glittering ornaments adorn trees ablaze in lights, store windows fill with holiday displays in red and green, and dreams of a white and icy-blue Christmas abound. So our last chapter, "Fancy Decorated Cookies," reflects the Christmas spirit of decking the halls, trimming the tree, and wrapping the gifts. Every Christmas at the Bakehouse we design new giant decorated cookies, like Norwegian sweater sets and friendly snowmen, and three-dimensional cookies such as the gingerbread fireplace and

house. As usual, we try to add a whimsical flair whenever possible. This lighthearted approach entices you to have fun and let the kid inside come out—and hey, why not let the real kids join in, too? You'll find that the decorating techniques here vary in difficulty, but we have made note of simpler alternative decorations wherever applicable.

Although we are professional bakers, neither my mom nor I had any professional training, and to make perfect holiday cookies, you don't need it either. Every recipe found on these pages is homespun. All of the ingredients and tools you need to bake and decorate are easily purchased from your local grocery store, craft store, or baker's supply store, or via the Internet. And we have prepared and tested all of the recipes using standard home equipment.

Making Christmas cookies is truly a labor of love. And the love you mix in will be returned tenfold by the smiles and cheers you will receive from your friends and family when they taste your creations!

—LIV HANSEN

getting started

THE TOOLS YOU WILL NEED TO GET STARTED depend on how elaborate your cookies are going to be. If you are planning on making recipes marked "easy," all you really need is an electric mixer, a rubber spatula, measuring cups and spoons, and a cookie sheet. If you bake cookies often or would like to make fancier cookies, you'll find the baking tools listed on the following pages useful. If you'll be decorating your cookies, be sure to check out the "Special Ingredients for Decorating" section. Almost everything on these lists can be found in your local supermarket or cookware shop, but if you can't find it there, see our list of suppliers on page 95.

tools of the trade

CARDBOARD * When we don't have the appropriate cookie cutter, or we want to make giant shaped cookies, we simply cut templates out of corrugated cardboard using an X-Acto or matte knife. Cardboard is more durable than paper and won't get destroyed when you run a knife along its edge to cut out cookies. (We have provided some templates on page 92.)

CELLOPHANE * We like to make our pastry cones out of cellophane instead of parchment paper because they hold up well in the microwave and maintain a clean, sharp point as you work. Cut rolls of cellophane into 10-inch squares or 5 × 10-inch rectangles. Hold the far right corner between your middle and index fingers and turn your hand toward the center; a point should begin to form at the center line. Continue this motion while wrapping the far left point around, pulling up on the far left point to form a sharp point at the tip of the cone. Apply a piece of tape close to the base to maintain the cone shape. Cellophane is also a great surface on which to pipe out chocolate decorations. Parchment will work fine as a substitute. For decoratively wrapping cookies, just use a length of cellophane, accented with a holiday ribbon.

COOKIE CUTTER * Cookie cutters come in all shapes and sizes, in plastic or metal, with a handle or without. Avoid cookie cutters that are shallow and have plastic or metal partially enclosing the top. Instead, we recommend fully open cutters because the dough releases with greater ease.

COOKIE SHEET * Standard cookie sheets measure 12¾ × 16½ inches on the inside (17¾ × 13 inches on the outside) and have either a shallow edge or no edge. Unless otherwise noted, this is the size pan to use for all of these recipes. We recommend medium- to heavy-gauge metal cookie sheets. A nonstick surface is not necessary, since we recommend greasing the pans or baking cookies on parchment paper.

ELECTRIC MIXER * This modern convenience is very handy for mixing up large batches of dough. Any brand will do, but we recommend the reliable 5-quart Kitchen-Aid. Handheld mixers also get the job done.

PAINTBRUSH * Soft sable or acrylic brushes are used to apply luster dusts onto hardened chocolate decorations. They can also be used to paint with melted chocolate.

PARCHMENT PAPER * This versatile paper is similar to wax paper, but without the wax coating. Use it to line cookie sheets to prevent baked goods from sticking. Chocolate doesn't stick to parchment paper either, so any chocolate design, no matter how delicate, can be piped onto it. You can also use parchment to make pastry cones. Just cut a 10-inch square diagonally in half to form two right triangles. With the 90-degree angle facing you, hold the two opposite corners and curl them toward the right angle. Overlapping one side over the other, pull one point around until it lines up with the other. Fold the points in, and apply a piece of tape close to the base to hold the cone's shape.

PASTRY BAG * These cone-shaped bags make piping doughs and decorations a breeze. We recommend 12- or 14-inch polyester bags, which can be washed and reused. Disposable ones are available, but they are not as strong. In a pinch, you can always fashion a bag out of a sheet of cellophane or parchment paper (see left). Plastic couplers are a very useful accessory. The coupler allows you to change tips with ease. It fits inside the pastry bag, while the tip goes on the outside, attached by a plastic ring. As an alternative, you can place a tip directly inside a bag without a coupler; just make sure the hole is not too big, or the tip will slip right out.

PASTRY CONE * See cellophane or parchment paper.

ROLLING PIN * Rolling pins come in many sizes, shapes, and materials. We recommend a wooden rolling pin with handles, measuring approximately 15 inches from end to end.

SILPAT * We have fallen in love with this alternative to parchment paper. This reusable silicone sheet is used to line cookie sheets. It cleans easily and cookies don't stick to it. Most cookies, with the exception of bar cookies, can be baked on a Silpat.

SPATULA (METAL AND RUBBER) * Spatulas come in all shapes and sizes. The thin, wide-bladed utensils are ideal for removing cookies from their sheet pans. Small offset spatulas, which we refer to at the Bakehouse as "baby bents," are great for spreading royal icing on cookies or for any other small and delicate task. A rubber spatula is essential for baking. Keep several handy for scraping down your mixing bowl and mixing colors into royal icing or white wafer chocolate.

SPRINGERLE MOLD * These cookie stamps or molds are made of carved wood or of porcelain lined with rubber. They are embossed with a variety of images that are transferred by pressing firmly into cookie dough.

SPRITZ MACHINE * There are numerous variations on this simple handheld machine, which creates the unique ridged cookies sold in many bakeries. For manual-powered machines, you fill the canister with soft cookie dough and then shape cookies either by squeezing the handle or twisting the top. Electric-powered versions tend to work better than the manual presses, although they cost a bit more. Different cookie designs can be created by changing the die in both types of spritz machines.

WIRE RACK * Wire racks are used to cool cookies, but if you've used parchment paper to line the cookie sheet, simply place the pan itself on the rack to cool; removing the hot cookies from the sheet and placing them directly on the rack can ruin some of your more delicate cookies. If you're using a greased pan instead, gently loosen the cookies with a spatula after they have cooled for 5 minutes, and remove to a rack to cool.

DRAGÉES * Used sparingly, these hard, round, metallic candies add sophisticated sparkle to any cookie. Dragées will adhere to unbaked cookie dough, soft royal icing, or melted chocolate.

FOOD COLORING * We like liquid gel colors (a professional product) because they add truly vivid hues to royal icing and cookie dough. They are sold at most high-end baking supply stores or through mail order (see "Suppliers," page 95). However, paste colors, which are more readily available, work perfectly well, too. For coloring wafer chocolate (see page 16), we use "candy colors," which are found at candy supply stores and craft stores or from mail-order sources.

LUSTER DUSTS * These edible metallic powders add an opulent glow when mixed with oil or liqueur, and can be painted onto smooth surfaces such as chilled ganache. They can also be dusted onto chocolate using a paint brush.

MERINGUE POWDER * We recommend meringue powder instead of egg whites for royal icing. It whips up more consistently and you don't have to worry about the bacteria sometimes found in raw eggs. If you would rather use egg whites, look for the pasteurized kind, which usually come frozen at most supermarkets. Meringue powder can also be found at your local supermarket or through specialty baking stores.

SANDING SUGAR * This coarse granulated sugar comes in a wide variety of colors. It effortlessly adds a festive touch when sprinkled on top of plain cookies. When sprinkled on cookies topped with royal icing, beautiful, glistening effects can be achieved.

SPRINKLES/NONPAREILS * These little beads of color are perfect for making any cookie festive and fun. You can even mix them into cookie dough for speckled treats.

WAFER CHOCOLATE * Wafer chocolate is actually not chocolate; it is a candy coating also known as confectioners' chocolate. It is easier to work with than chocolate because it does not need to be tempered (so it stays shiny when it resolidifies after being melted) and it has a lower melting point. It comes in dark chocolate, white chocolate, and a limited range of colors. If you can't find wafer chocolate, you can substitute Baker's Dipping Chocolate, which is more readily available in grocery stores. For more information on decorating with chocolate, see page 67.

baking tips

For every cookie recipe, make sure you have all of the ingredients and equipment you need before you start. It's also a good idea to familiarize yourself with the recipe by giving it a read-through before you begin.

Below are some additional useful hints. We know they'll help you bake even more delicious goodies!

* Always remember to preheat your oven. This will help the cookies bake properly.

* Carefully measure all of your ingredients, using dry-ingredient measuring cups and liquid measuring cups as needed. Remember: Baking is like a science. It requires accuracy.

* Unless otherwise noted, it is important to have your ingredients, especially your butter and eggs, at room temperature. This will facilitate the creaming and mixing of the dough.

* Adding too much flour in the hope of firming up a sticky batch of dough will only make it tough. Instead, try chilling the dough.

* Always remember to scrape down your mixing bowl often, being careful to get all the way to the bottom of the bowl where sometimes the electric-mixer paddle or whip does not reach. This will ensure that all of the ingredients are well combined.

* Most cookie doughs can be prepared well ahead of their baking time. Simply wrap the dough in plastic wrap and either refrigerate or freeze it until you are ready to cut or roll it out. If sealed well, cookie dough can last up to one month in your freezer.

* Remember, most cookies have a rather long shelf life—up to two weeks. Even bar cookies, if wrapped in plastic wrap, will have an extended shelf life. Some cookies can be frozen after baking and, if sealed well, can last up to two months. So don't be afraid to start your holiday baking early.

* When making oversize rolled-out cookies, we recommend rolling out the dough, chilling it, and then cutting out your cookies. Your cookies will have neater edges.

* A good rule of thumb when baking for a crowd is one pound of cookies for every eight to ten people. One pound, depending on the weight of each cookie, is about twenty-five to thirty-five cookies.

simple decorating tips

It's easy to transform almost any cookie into a Christmas cookie. Just adding hints of color (especially red and green) or a simple decoration can breathe new life into a normally sedate cookie. The following list includes some quick ideas for making your cookies truly festive.

* Sprinkle the tops of your cookies with pretty colored sanding sugar or nonpareils before baking.

* Roll the log of cookie dough in sanding sugar before slicing and baking.

* Use holiday-themed cookie cutters to transform basic, rolled-out cookie dough into fancy Christmas treats. Just cut and bake—voilà.

* Drizzle the tops of your baked cookies with dark or tinted white chocolate. Or drizzle the tops with chocolate and then, before the chocolate has hardened, sprinkle with sanding sugar or nonpareils.

* Replace chocolate chips in any cookie recipe with colored candy-coated chocolate chips.

* Mix sprinkles and nonpareils thoroughly into shortbread or plain butter cookie dough for a multicolored explosion.

* Use color! Of course, the traditional colors of Christmas are red and green, but don't feel bound to just those two. Try using the icy blues and pastels that are so reminiscent of a snowy day. Silver and gold are just as appropriate for this season. You can gild everything from chocolate star cookies to ornament-shaped ones. If you can't find luster dusts, try dragées for a sophisticated sparkle.

how to temper chocolate

Find a metal bowl that fits snuggly in a medium-size pot, or use a double boiler. Coarsely chop the chocolate and place three-fourths of it in the bowl. Fill the pot one-third full with water and bring it to a boil. Remove the pot from the heat and place the bowl on top; do not let the bottom of the bowl touch the water. Heat the chocolate, while stirring, until a thermometer reads 118 to 120°F. for semisweet chocolate or 116 to 118°F. for milk chocolate. Remove the bowl from the heat. Add the remaining chocolate and stir until the thermometer reads 80°F. Bring the water in the pot to a boil again, remove it from the heat, and once again place the bowl of chocolate on top. Reheat the chocolate, stirring, until a thermometer reads 88 to 91°F. for semisweet chocolate or 85 to 87°F. for milk chocolate. Keep the chocolate at this temperature until you use it.

A NOTE ON WRAPPING COOKIES

If you are giving cookies as a gift, arrange them, layered with wax paper or parchment paper, in holiday tins or in boxes tied with ribbon. Clear and holiday-décor cellophane bags (available at craft stores or party supply stores) also make a wonderful display for your baked goods. Just tie the package with a length of your favorite ribbon. (For more fragile types of cookies, insert a cardboard liner for support.)

hand-formed cookies

You don't need a rolling pin or any fancy gadgets to shape these easy cookies—just your hands. The decorations, likewise, are simple touches: A dollop of ruby-red raspberry jam, a sprinkling of sanding sugar, or a dusting of confectioners' sugar is all the decoration these delectable treats need. You will find a wide range of flavors, too—not only the Christmas standards of sugar, butter, nuts, and cinnamon, but also more exotic ones like macadamia, espresso, and coconut. We hope you enjoy baking these gems as much as you and your friends and family will enjoy eating them.

creamy christmas butter cookies

When we first sampled these cookies, we couldn't believe our taste buds. Their simple buttery goodness just screamed "Christmas." And as far as time and energy go, you can't get much easier than this cookie. For decoration all you need to do is imprint each cookie with a fork and sprinkle the tops with green or red sanding sugar before baking. 🎄

* * MAKES 4 DOZEN COOKIES * *

Preheat the oven to 350°F.

Grease 2 cookie sheets.

In a large bowl of an electric mixer at medium speed, mix just until blended:

> 8 ounces (2 sticks) unsalted butter, softened
> 1½ cups confectioners' sugar
> 1 teaspoon vanilla extract

Add and mix well:

> 1 large egg

In a separate bowl, mix together:

> 2¼ cups all-purpose flour
> 1 teaspoon baking soda
> 1 teaspoon cream of tartar
> ¼ teaspoon salt

Add to the butter mixture and mix at low speed until well combined.

Have on hand:

> Colored sanding sugar

Shape the dough into ¾-inch balls. Arrange the balls 2 inches apart on the cookie sheets. Flatten each ball with a fork (to prevent your fork from sticking to the cookie dough, dip it occasionally in confectioners' sugar). Sprinkle the tops of the cookies with colored sanding sugar. Bake for 8 to 10 minutes, or until lightly colored around the edges. Let the cookies cool in the pans for 5 minutes, then transfer the cookies to a wire rack to cool completely.

candy canes

These are delightful and easy-to-make cookies that are colored, rolled, and formed to look like real candy canes. At the Bakehouse we like to make giant cookie candy canes, wrap them in cellophane, and tie them with a bow to create the perfect stocking stuffer or gift. 🎄

· · · MAKES 9 LARGE CANDY CANES · · ·

Preheat the oven to 350°F.

Grease 2 cookie sheets.

In a large bowl of an electric mixer at medium speed, cream:

> 8 ounces (2 sticks) unsalted butter, softened
> 1 cup confectioners' sugar
> 1 large egg
> 1 teaspoon almond extract
> 1 teaspoon vanilla extract

Add and mix at low speed until well combined:

> 2½ cups all-purpose flour
> 1 teaspoon salt

Remove half of the dough from the mixing bowl. To the remaining dough, add:

> 5 drops red food coloring (or enough food coloring to make the dough red)

Mix until well combined.

Divide the red and the uncolored dough into 9 equal pieces. On a board, roll 1 piece of each kind of dough into logs of equal length (approximately 9 inches). If the dough begins to stick, sprinkle the board with a little confectioners' sugar. Repeat with the remaining dough. Chill the logs for 10 minutes. Place 2 logs (1 red, 1 white) side by side and lightly twist together. Curve the top to form a cane. Repeat with the remaining logs.

Arrange the candy canes 2 inches apart on the cookie sheets. Bake for 12 to 15 minutes, or until lightly colored. Let the cookies cool in the pans for 5 minutes, then transfer the cookies to a wire rack to cool completely.

NOTE *Their candy cane shape makes these cookies prone to breaking, but wrapped securely they should travel well.*

chocolate krinkle cookies

This recipe comes from Liv's sister-in-law, Sandy, who bakes them every year for Christmas. The name reminds us of Kris Kringle, so we're sure Santa would love a plate of krinkles waiting for him on your mantelpiece. The balls of cookie dough are rolled in confectioners' sugar, which creates a cracked-sugar surface once they're baked. The crispy, snow-topped exterior conceals an unexpectedly yummy and gooey middle. 🎄

* * MAKES 6 DOZEN COOKIES * *

In a large bowl of an electric mixer at medium speed, cream:

    2 *cups granulated sugar*

    ³⁄₄ *cup vegetable oil or* ¹⁄₂ *cup clarified butter and* ¹⁄₄ *cup vegetable oil*

Add and mix at low speed until well combined:

    ³⁄₄ *cup cocoa powder*

Add and beat until well combined:

    4 *large eggs*

    2 *teaspoons vanilla extract*

On a piece of parchment paper, sift together:

    2¹⁄₃ *cups all-purpose flour*

    2 *teaspoons baking powder*

    ¹⁄₂ *teaspoon salt*

Add to the sugar mixture and mix at low speed until combined.

Cover the soft dough with plastic wrap and chill for 6 hours or overnight.

Set aside:

    1 *cup sifted confectioners' sugar*

Preheat the oven to 350°F.

Grease 2 cookie sheets.

Roll the dough into 1-inch balls. Roll each ball in confectioners' sugar and arrange them 1 inch apart on the cookie sheets. Bake for 12 to 14 minutes, or until the cookies have puffed up slightly. Let the cookies cool in the pans for 5 minutes, then transfer the cookies to a wire rack to cool completely.

pecan snowballs

Reminiscent of real snowballs, these tender cookies really do melt in your mouth. Roll the dough into balls; they retain their round shape when baked. Coating the cookies plentifully in confectioners' sugar after baking completes the illusion of snowballs. 🌲

* * MAKES 4 DOZEN COOKIES * *

Preheat the oven to 350°F.

Line 2 cookie sheets with parchment paper.

On a sheet pan, toast for 8 to 10 minutes or until fragrant:

   3 ounces (¾ cup) whole pecans

When the pecans are cool, chop them into medium-coarse pieces, and set aside.

In a large bowl of an electric mixer at low speed, mix well:

   8 ounces (2 sticks) unsalted butter, softened
   ½ cup confectioners' sugar
   1 teaspoon vanilla extract
   ¼ teaspoon salt

Add and mix at low speed until well combined:

   2¼ cups all-purpose flour
   the chopped pecans

Roll the dough into ¾-inch balls. Arrange the balls 1 inch apart on the cookie sheets. Bake for 10 to 12 minutes, or until the undersides are a very pale brown. Roll the cookies in additional confectioners' sugar while they are still warm.

nutty thumbprint cookies

This is an adaptation from a booklet called *Christmas Cookies from Around the World* that I found in a package of Pillsbury flour more than thirty years ago. First rolled in nuts then imprinted with your thumb, they look very festive when raspberry or apricot jam is piped in the center. Be careful when packing these cookies—let the jam set before stacking them. ♣

Preheat the oven to 350°F.

Grease 2 cookie sheets.

Finely chop and set aside:

    6 ounces (1½ cups) walnuts

Stir until smooth and set aside:

    2 cups seedless raspberry jam

In a large bowl of an electric mixer at medium speed, beat until blended:

    6 ounces (1½ sticks) unsalted butter, softened

    2 large egg yolks (reserve whites)

    ¾ cup sugar

    ½ teaspoon vanilla extract

    ½ teaspoon almond extract

    ½ teaspoon salt

Add and mix at low speed until well combined:

    2 cups all-purpose flour

In a small bowl, lightly whisk the reserved egg whites. Spread the reserved chopped nuts on a plate. Roll the dough into 1-inch balls. Dip each ball in the egg whites, then roll it in the chopped nuts. Arrange the balls 1 inch apart on the cookie sheets. Make a deep impression in the center of each with your finger (or a wooden spoon handle). Bake for 10 to 12 minutes, or until the bottoms are golden brown; do not overbake.

While the cookies are still warm, fill a pastry bag with the raspberry jam. Fill each cookie with a heaping dollop of jam. Let the cookies cool in the pans for 5 minutes, then transfer the cookies to a wire rack to cool completely.

walnut acorns

At the bakery, we know Christmas is on its way when the smell of Walnut Acorns fills the air. Perhaps it is the rich, nutty aroma that reminds us of the holiday. They are also remarkably easy to make: You don't even need a mixer, just a saucepan and a wooden spoon. Kids will love to join in with shaping and dipping the cookies and, of course, eating them, too. 🌲

* * MAKES 4 DOZEN COOKIES * *

Preheat the oven to 350°F.

Grease 2 cookie sheets.

In a medium saucepan over low heat, melt together:

> 8 ounces (2 sticks) unsalted butter
> ¾ cup dark brown sugar, packed

Whisk over heat until smooth. Remove from the heat and let cool for 10 minutes.

Add:

> 1 teaspoon vanilla extract

Combine and stir into butter mixture:

> 2⅓ cups all-purpose flour
> ½ teaspoon baking powder
> 3 ounces (¾ cup) chopped walnuts

Mold a heaping mound of dough onto a teaspoon and press the dough firmly with the palm of your hand to form a rounded "acorn" shape. Gently slide the shaped dough off of the spoon and onto the cookie sheet. Repeat to form the remaining cookies, spacing them 1 inch apart on the cookie sheets. Bake for 10 to 15 minutes, or until the undersides are lightly browned; do not overbake. Let the cookies cool in the pans for 5 minutes, then transfer the cookies to a wire rack to cool completely.

Melt:

> 12 ounces semisweet chocolate

Finely chop:

> 4 ounces (1 cup) walnuts

Dip half of each cookie into the melted chocolate, and then into the nuts. Stir the nuts often so they don't clump, ensuring that they adhere more readily to the chocolate. Arrange the cookies on a large piece of parchment paper to set.

coconut dreams

Christmas in upstate New York can be frigidly cold, so we often find ourselves dreaming of the holidays in the tropics. To bring a little of that warmth to your table, try these treats redolent of toasted pecans and coconut. Even people who don't love nuts can't get enough of these cookies. ♣

Preheat the oven to 350°F.

Grease 2 cookie sheets.

On a sheet pan, toast for 8 to 10 minutes, or until fragrant:

1½ ounces (⅓ cup) whole pecans

When the pecans are cool, chop them into medium-coarse pieces, and set aside.

In a large bowl of an electric mixer at medium speed, cream:

6 ounces (1½ sticks) unsalted butter, softened

¾ cup light brown sugar, packed

⅓ cup granulated sugar

1 teaspoon vanilla extract

In a separate bowl, mix together:

1½ cups all-purpose flour

¾ teaspoon baking soda

⅛ teaspoon salt

Add to the butter mixture and mix at low speed until a soft dough forms.

Add and mix at low speed, just until combined:

the chopped pecans

Chop in a food processor and spread on a wide plate:

1½ cups shredded sweetened coconut

Roll mounded teaspoonfuls of dough into balls. Roll each ball in the chopped coconut. Place the balls 2 inches apart on the cookie sheets. Bake for 8 to 12 minutes, or until they are just starting to color. Let the cookies cool in the pans for 5 minutes, then transfer the cookies to a wire rack to cool completely.

cinnamon springerle cookies

Springerle cookies have been the traditional Christmas cookies of Bavaria for centuries. These edible works of art are beautiful enough to hang on your tree or give as a gift. We found a wonderful large poinsettia stamp that works perfectly. Although springerle is traditionally flavored with anise, we prefer to use cinnamon. Springerle molds can be purchased through The Baker's Catalogue, on the Internet, or in stores like Williams-Sonoma. ✦

✶ ✷ MAKES 1 ½ DOZEN LARGE COOKIES ✷ ✶

Preheat the oven to 350°F.

Grease 2 cookie sheets.

In a large bowl of an electric mixer at medium speed, cream:

> 8 ounces (2 sticks) unsalted butter, softened
> 1 cup sugar

Add and cream:

> 1 large egg

In a separate bowl, mix together:

> 2¼ cups all-purpose flour
> 1 tablespoon cinnamon

Add to the butter mixture and mix at low speed until well combined.

In a small bowl, set aside:

> ¾ cup sugar

Roll the dough into 18 golf-ball-size balls (or even smaller depending on the size of your cookie stamp). Roll each ball in the sugar. Arrange them 3 inches apart on the cookie sheets. Dip the stamp in sugar. Center the stamp over each cookie and press down firmly until you see the sides of the dough on the outer edge. Lift off the stamp and repeat with the remaining balls of dough. Bake for 12 to 15 minutes, or until golden brown. Let the cookies cool in the pans for 5 minutes, then transfer the cookies to a wire rack to cool completely.

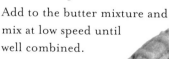

chocolate espresso balls

Who doesn't need a little jolt of energy during the hectic holidays? These bite-size treats will give you just that. Indulge yourself with these dense, crumbly cookies that are packed with chocolate and espresso flavor and lightly dusted with cocoa powder and confectioners' sugar. 🌲

* * MAKES 6 DOZEN COOKIES * *

Preheat the oven to 350°F.

Line 2 cookie sheets with parchment paper.

On a sheet pan, toast for 8 to 10 minutes or until fragrant:

    4 ounces (1 cup) whole pecans

When the pecans are cool, chop them into medium-fine pieces, and set aside.

In a large bowl of an electric mixer, cream:

    8 ounces (2 sticks) unsalted butter, softened
    ⅔ cup dark brown sugar, firmly packed
    ¼ teaspoon salt

Add and cream:

    2 large egg yolks
    1 teaspoon vanilla extract

Add and mix at low speed until well combined:

    ⅓ cup cocoa powder
    2 cups all-purpose flour
    1 tablespoon espresso powder

Add the toasted pecans.

Sift together and set aside:

    ⅓ cup cocoa powder
    1 cup confectioners' sugar

Roll the dough into ¾-inch balls. Arrange them 1 inch apart on the cookie sheets. Bake for 10 to 12 minutes, or until firm and dry to the touch. Roll the cookies in the cocoa powder–sugar mixture while they are still warm.

macadamia brittle cookies

An exotic twist on almond praline, these macadamia brittle cookies have a luxurious Christmassy richness. They are well worth the extra step of making the praline, especially since it can be done a day ahead. Consider making a double batch: They make a great Christmas gift. 🌲🌲

Line a cookie sheet with parchment paper.

✳ PRALINE:

Preheat the oven to 350°F.

On a sheet pan, toast for 8 to 10 minutes or until fragrant:

8 ounces (1¾ cups) macadamia nuts

When the macadamia nuts are cool, coarsely chop them, and set aside.

In a heavy saucepan, cook over moderate heat:

⅔ cup sugar

Shake the saucepan 2 or 3 times until the sugar melts, then cook without stirring until the sugar becomes caramel colored. Remove from the heat and add ½ cup of the toasted macadamia nuts (reserve the remaining nuts). Pour the praline nut mixture onto the prepared cookie sheet and let cool completely.

✳ COOKIE DOUGH:

Grease 2 cookie sheets.

Break apart the praline into pieces and grind in a food processor.

Add the remaining toasted macadamia nuts. Continue grinding until medium fine.

In a large bowl of an electric mixer at medium speed, cream:

8 ounces (2 sticks) unsalted butter, softened
½ cup confectioners' sugar

Add:

2¼ cups all-purpose flour
the praline mixture

Roll tablespoonfuls of dough into 2½-inch logs. Arrange them 1 inch apart on the cookie sheets and flatten each log slightly. Bake for 8 to 10 minutes, or until lightly colored. Let the cookies cool in the pans for

5 minutes, then transfer the cookies to a wire rack to cool completely.

Melt separately:

> 2   cups dark wafer chocolate or
>   12 ounces semisweet chocolate
>   (tempered, see page 19)
> ½ cup white wafer chocolate or 3 ounces
>   white chocolate

Dip one end of each cookie in the melted
dark chocolate and let dry on a piece of
parchment paper. Drizzle the tops with
white chocolate.

> VARIATION ✳ *Instead of plain white
> chocolate, drizzle the chocolate-dipped cookies
> with ½ cup white wafer chocolate, melted and
> tinted with red and green candy colors.*

seasonal sliced cookies

Our "icebox" cookies are almost as convenient as the slice-and-bake cookies found in the refrigerated aisle of your grocery store, but ours definitely are more delicious. The cookie dough, when wrapped in a log, can be frozen for up to a month. Whenever you have a craving for sweets, or you have unexpected guests, just thaw, slice, and bake. We think the easiest way to embellish the cookies is to roll the fresh cookie dough logs in colored sanding sugar for sparkle or nonpareils for a whimsical flair. A touch of glistening white, crimson, or evergreen is often all you need to create a Christmas feeling.

orange sablés

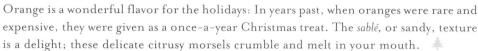

Orange is a wonderful flavor for the holidays: In years past, when oranges were rare and expensive, they were given as a once-a-year Christmas treat. The *sablé*, or sandy, texture is a delight; these delicate citrusy morsels crumble and melt in your mouth. 🎄

* * MAKES 4 TO 5 DOZEN COOKIES * *

In a large bowl of an electric mixer at medium speed, beat to combine:

> 8 ounces (2 sticks) unsalted butter, softened
>
> ¾ cup confectioners' sugar

In a separate bowl, mix together:

> 1½ cups all-purpose flour
>
> ¾ cup cornstarch

Add to the butter mixture and mix at low speed until a soft dough forms.

Add and mix at low speed until well combined:

> 1 tablespoon grated orange zest
>
> 1 teaspoon vanilla extract

Set aside:

> 1 cup colored sanding sugar

On a clean board, roll the dough into two 9-inch logs. Pour the sanding sugar onto a cookie sheet. Roll each log in the colored sanding sugar. Wrap each log in plastic and chill for 8 hours or overnight.

When you are ready to bake the sablés, preheat the oven to 350°F. Grease 2 cookie sheets.

Cut the chilled dough into ¼-inch slices and arrange them 1 inch apart on the cookie sheets. Bake for 12 to 16 minutes, or until lightly colored. Let the cookies cool in the pans for 5 minutes, then transfer the cookies to a wire rack to cool completely.

lemon drop cookies

After all the heavy meals eaten during the holidays, a refreshing dessert is just what you need. Here the tang of lemon and the sweetness of almond balance each other beautifully, making cookies that are delicate yet rich in flavor at the same time. This recipe is an adaptation of our popular lemon tart from the Bakehouse. We use the walnut almond dough from the lemon tart's crust as a cookie dough, and pipe the lemon curd filling into the center of each.

This recipe makes enough lemon curd to top two batches of cookies, or top one batch and use the remainder as the filling for a lemon tart. 🌲🌲

✳✳ MAKES 3 DOZEN COOKIES ✳✳

✳ LEMON CURD:

In a saucepan, bring to a boil:

> 1 *tablespoon grated lemon zest*
> ½ *cup strained fresh lemon juice*
> ½ *cup sugar*
> 3 *ounces (¾ stick) unsalted butter*

In a large bowl of an electric mixer at medium speed, beat well:

> 4 *large eggs*

Slowly whisk the hot juice mixture into the eggs. Return the mixture to the saucepan and cook over medium-low heat until the curd coats the back of a spoon. Do not let the mixture boil or it will curdle. Pour the curd through a strainer into a bowl. Place plastic wrap directly on the surface of the curd and refrigerate until cold. To chill the curd quickly, place the bowl over a bowl of ice and stir until cold.

* COOKIE DOUGH:

In a large bowl of an electric mixer at medium speed, beat to combine, but do not cream:

> 5 ounces (1¼ sticks) unsalted butter, softened
> ¾ cup sugar

Mix in until just combined:

> 1 large egg yolk
> 2 teaspoons grated lemon zest
> ¼ teaspoon almond extract

In a separate bowl, mix together:

> 1¼ cups all-purpose flour
> ⅛ teaspoon salt
> 2½ ounces (½ cup) medium-fine-chopped almonds
> 1 ounce (¼ cup) medium-fine-chopped walnuts

Add to the butter mixture and mix at low speed until a soft dough forms.

On a lightly floured board, roll the dough into two 10-inch logs. Wrap each log in plastic and chill for 8 hours or overnight.

When you are ready to bake the cookies, preheat the oven to 350°F. Grease 2 cookie sheets.

Cut the chilled dough into ¼-inch slices and arrange them 2 inches apart on the cookie sheets. Place lemon curd into a pastry bag with a small (#8) round tip. Pipe a small dollop of lemon curd onto the center of each cookie. Bake for 12 to 16 minutes, or until lightly colored. Let the cookies cool in the pans for 5 minutes, then transfer the cookies to a wire rack to cool completely.

pistachio gems

Like sparkling gems, these cookies are pretty enough to hang on your tree. To get the bejeweled effect, we dip each cookie in melted white chocolate and then in colorful sanding sugar. The hints of green from the chopped pistachios show up so beautifully that these cookies can even go unadorned. 🌲

✶ ✶ MAKES 4 TO 6 DOZEN COOKIES ✶ ✶

In a large bowl of an electric mixer at medium speed, beat until just combined:

> 8 ounces (2 sticks) unsalted butter, softened
>
> ½ cup light brown sugar, packed

Add and blend in:

> 2 cups plus 2 tablespoons all-purpose flour
>
> 2½ ounces (½ cup) coarsely chopped pistachios
>
> ¼ teaspoon almond extract
>
> ¼ teaspoon vanilla extract

Roll the dough into two 10-inch logs. Wrap in plastic and chill for 8 hours or overnight.

When you are ready to bake the cookies, preheat the oven to 350°F. Grease 2 cookie sheets.

Cut the chilled dough into ¼-inch slices and arrange them 1 inch apart on the cookie sheets. Bake for 8 to 12 minutes, or until edges are lightly colored. Let the cookies cool in the pans for 5 minutes, then transfer the cookies to a wire rack to cool completely.

In a small bowl, set aside:

> ½ cup each green and red sanding sugar

Melt:

> 2 cups white wafer chocolate or 12 ounces white chocolate

Dip half of each cookie in the melted chocolate, then in green or red sanding sugar. Allow the cookies to set on parchment paper.

rich butter cookies with glacé cherries

The translucent glow of glacé cherries reminds us of shimmering Christmas lights, so we decorated these festive cookies with half of a cherry. But the greatest attribute of these simple cookies is their rich buttery flavor. 🌲

* * MAKES 6 DOZEN COOKIES * *

In a large bowl of an electric mixer at medium speed, beat together:

  1 *pound (4 sticks) unsalted butter, softened*
  3 *cups confectioners' sugar*

Add to the butter mixture and beat until fluffy:

  2 *large eggs*
  1 *teaspoon vanilla extract*

Add to the butter mixture and mix at low speed until a soft dough forms:

  5 *cups all-purpose flour*

Divide the dough into 4 equal pieces. Roll each piece into a 9-inch-long log. Wrap each log in plastic and chill for 8 hours or overnight.

When you are ready to bake the cookies, preheat the oven to 350° F. Grease 2 cookie sheets.

Cut in half and set aside:

  36 *glacé cherries*

Cut the chilled logs into ¼-inch slices. Place the slices on the cookie sheets 1 inch apart.

In the center of each slice, gently press a glacé cherry half. Bake for 8 to 12 minutes, or until edges are lightly colored. Let the cookies cool in the pans for 5 minutes, then transfer the cookies to a wire rack to cool completely.

VARIATION ✳ *If you aren't the biggest fan of cherries, just bake these cookies with a whole walnut pressed into each slice of cookie dough. It lends the cookie an earthy elegance.*

tricolor cookies

Whimsical swirls and checkerboards of red, green, and white make these lighthearted Christmas cookies a joy to see and eat. By simply tinting the dough, then stacking, rolling, and slicing, even the novice decorator can get gorgeous, fun results. If you're short on time, pick the spiral design. This classic Christmas sugar cookie dough is a favorite with children of all ages. 🌲🌲

* * MAKES 4 DOZEN COOKIES * *

In a large bowl of an electric mixer at medium speed, cream:

> 8 ounces (2 sticks) unsalted butter, softened
>
> 1½ cups confectioners' sugar
>
> 1 large egg
>
> 1 teaspoon vanilla extract

Add and mix at low speed until well combined:

> 2½ cups all-purpose flour
>
> 1 teaspoon baking soda
>
> 1 teaspoon cream of tartar
>
> ¼ teaspoon salt

Have on hand:

> Red and green food coloring (see Note)

Whisk and set aside:

> 1 egg

Remove one-third of the dough and tint it red by kneading a few drops at a time of red liquid gel or paste color into the dough until you have the desired color. Remove another third of the dough and tint it green in the same manner. Keep the remaining dough uncolored. Chill the dough for 30 minutes.

For a spiral: On a lightly floured board, roll each color of dough out to a rectangle of equal size, ¼ inch thick. Lightly brush the red dough with the beaten egg, being careful to leave no puddles. Stack the green rectangle directly on top of the red one, pressing lightly to adhere. Brush the green layer with the beaten egg and stack the white layer on top. Press lightly to adhere. Roll lengthwise into a tight log. Wrap the log in plastic wrap and chill for 8 hours or overnight.

For a checkerboard: On a lightly floured board, roll the red and green balls of dough out into 3 × 12-inch rectangles, ⅓ inch thick. Lightly brush the red dough with the beaten egg, being careful to leave no puddles. Stack the green rectangle directly on top of the red. Cut this stack lengthwise into two equal strips. Lightly brush one strip with beaten egg and lay the other strip on top so that the colors alternate. Wrap in plastic and chill until firm. When the stack has set, cut it lengthwise into four equal strips. Roll out the white dough to the length of the strips, and wide enough to wrap around it (about 7 × 12 inches) and approximately ⅛ inch thick. Working atop a piece of parchment paper, lightly brush the white dough with beaten egg. Place one strip ½ inch in from one edge of the white dough. Brush this strip lightly with the beaten egg. Lay the second strip on top of the first strip so that the colors alternate. Repeat these steps with the remaining two strips. Press the edge of the white dough closest to the stack against the stack. Now, begin to roll the stack tightly along the white dough so that the white dough wraps around the stack completely. Keep the parchment paper in place until the white dough is adhered, all the way around, to the stack.

Wrap the log in plastic wrap and chill for 8 hours or overnight.

When you are ready to bake the cookies, preheat the oven to 350°F. Grease 2 cookie sheets.

Cut the log into ¼-inch slices and arrange them 1 inch apart on the cookie sheets. Bake for 8 to 10 minutes, or until lightly colored. Let the cookies cool in the pans for 5 minutes, then transfer the cookies to a wire rack to cool completely.

NOTE *The amount of dye needed to tint cookie dough depends largely on the brand and type of food coloring you decide to use. Liquid gel colors are slightly stronger than paste colors, and basic food coloring from the supermarket is even less concentrated. Use your judgment as to how rich you want the color. Remember to err on the side of caution by mixing in small amounts of dye at a time to ensure the dough does not get too dark. Keep in mind that the baked cookies will be slightly darker than the dough.*

yin-yang cookies

For those of you who celebrate the winter solstice in addition to Christmas, our New Age cookie is perfect. The balance of flavors and colors reflects the cycle of the seasons and of life. In these cookies, cherry-almond and chocolate-walnut cookie doughs off-set each other in a yin-yang swirl. Complete the decoration by piping white and dark chocolate dots on the opposing sides. 🌲 🌲

** MAKES 5 TO 6 DOZEN COOKIES **

* CHERRY-ALMOND DOUGH:

In a large bowl of an electric mixer at medium speed, cream:

> 6 ounces (1½ sticks) unsalted butter, softened
>
> 1 cup confectioners' sugar

Add at medium-low speed and blend well:

> 1 large egg
>
> 1 tablespoon fresh orange juice
>
> ¼ teaspoon almond extract

Add and mix at low speed until well combined:

> 1¾ cups all-purpose flour
>
> ½ cup dried cherries, chopped
>
> 2½ ounces (½ cup) blanched almonds, chopped

* CHOCOLATE-WALNUT DOUGH:

In the bowl of an electric mixer at medium speed, mix together:

> 8 ounces (2 sticks) unsalted butter, softened
>
> 1 cup confectioners' sugar
>
> ½ teaspoon vanilla extract

Add and mix at low speed until well combined:

> 1⅓ cups all-purpose flour
>
> ½ cup cocoa powder
>
> 4 ounces (1 cup) walnuts, chopped

On a lightly floured board, roll the 2 doughs into 4 logs each. Chill for 10 minutes. With a rolling pin, press down lengthwise on one-third of each log. Take 1 log of each type of dough, and connect the fat side of 1 log with the thin side of the other. Roll them together

until they adhere to each other and form 1 uniform log. Look at the side and see if the yin-yang form has appeared. If not, continue to roll the log until it does. Repeat with the remaining logs. Wrap the logs in plastic and chill for 8 hours or overnight.

When ready to bake, preheat the oven to 350°F. Grease 2 cookie sheets.

Cut the logs into ¼-inch slices and arrange them 1 inch apart on the cookie sheets. Bake for 10 to 12 minutes, or until lightly colored. Let the cookies cool in the pans for 5 minutes, then transfer the cookies to a wire rack to cool completely.

Melt:

> ½ cup white wafer chocolate
>   or 3 ounces white chocolate
> ½ cup dark wafer chocolate
>   or 3 ounces semisweet chocolate

Pour each chocolate into a pastry cone. Cut a small hole at the tip of each.

Pipe a white dot on the dark side and a dark dot on the light side of each cookie. Let the chocolate set.

piped cookies

Unlike the firmer hand-formed and sliced cookies, the cookies in this chapter are made with softer dough that is too sticky to form with your hands or roll out, so they are piped out with a pastry bag. We recommend using these doughs right away, since they are easier to pipe right after mixing. The decorations are still simple and magical: melted chocolate, nuts, sugar, and more.

raspberry spritz cookies

You may recognize these cookies, since look-alikes are found in almost every corner deli at this time of year—only these taste much better. To achieve the shaped and ridged effect, you need a spritz machine (sometimes called a cookie press). Most spritz machines come with a variety of disks with Christmas designs such as trees, wreaths, candy canes, and stars. 🌲🌲

* * MAKES 4 DOZEN COOKIES * *

Preheat the oven to 375°F.

In a large bowl of an electric mixer at medium speed, cream:

> 8 ounces (2 sticks) unsalted butter, softened
>
> 1 cup sugar

Add and mix at low speed until well combined:

> 1 large egg
>
> 1 teaspoon vanilla extract

Add and mix at low speed until a soft dough forms:

> 2¼ cups all-purpose flour
>
> ½ teaspoon salt
>
> ¼ teaspoon baking powder

Add and mix until combined:

> 1 teaspoon natural raspberry flavor

Have on hand, if desired:

> colored sanding sugars

Pack the dough into the cookie press.

Fit the press with the desired disk design and press the dough out onto an ungreased cookie sheet (do not use a nonstick pan) according to the instructions for your cookie press. Depending on your press, you will probably either hand twist or squeeze a handle until the desired size cookie is pressed out onto the sheet pan, then pull up to release the dough from the press. Sprinkle the cookies with sanding sugar if desired. Bake for 10 to 12 minutes, or until lightly colored. Let the cookies cool in the pans for 5 minutes, then transfer the cookies to a wire rack to cool completely.

NOTE *If you can't get your hands on a spritz machine, you can use a pastry bag with a star tip and simply pipe the dough out into circles. Sprinkle the tops with red and green sanding sugar, and they will look like Christmas wreaths when baked!*

chocolate pecan rounds

Your children won't mistake these delicious cookies for lumps of coal. These piped chocolate pecan cookies are sandwiched with white chocolate and raspberry jam, then drizzled with white chocolate. 🌲🌲

** MAKES 5 TO 6 DOZEN COOKIES **

Preheat the oven to 350°F.

Grease 2 cookie sheets.

In a food processor, grind until medium-fine:

    6 ounces (1½ cups) walnuts

    2 cups all-purpose flour

In a large bowl of an electric mixer at medium speed, cream:

    1 pound (4 sticks) unsalted butter, softened

  1½ cups granulated sugar

    1 cup confectioners' sugar

Add and cream:

    2 extra-large eggs

    2 teaspoons vanilla extract

On a piece of wax paper, sift together:

   ½ cup all-purpose flour

    1 cup cocoa powder

Add the walnut mixture and the flour mixture to the butter mixture and beat at low speed until well combined.

Place the dough in a pastry bag with a #12 round tip. On the cookie sheets, 1 inch apart, pipe the dough into 1-inch rounds. Bake for 10 to 12 minutes. Let the cookies cool in the pans for 5 minutes, then transfer the cookies to a wire rack to cool completely.

Stir until smooth:

    1 cup raspberry jam

Melt:

    1 cup white wafer chocolate or 6 to 8 ounces white chocolate

Place the raspberry jam in a pastry bag with a small round tip. Place the melted white chocolate in a pastry cone. Cut a medium-size hole at the tip. Turn half of the cookies upside down. Pipe a dollop of white chocolate and raspberry jam on each upturned half. Sandwich the halves together while the chocolate is still warm. Drizzle the tops of the cookies with the remaining white chocolate.

coconut macaroons

At the Bakehouse, we produce tons of macaroons for Chanukah, and because they are so popular we find ourselves making them right through Christmas—since our customers keep asking for them. They are the best macaroons you'll ever have, so sweet and addictive they are almost like candy. We dip ours halfway in chocolate. 🌲 🌲

** MAKES 6 TO 7 DOZEN COOKIES **

Preheat the oven to 450°F.

Grease 2 cookie sheets.

In a medium saucepan, melt:

    4 ounces (1 stick) unsalted butter

Add and stir together:

    1½ cups sugar

In a large bowl of an electric mixer, combine by hand:

    1¼ cups light corn syrup
    ½ teaspoon salt
    ½ teaspoon vanilla extract
    1 cup plus 2 tablespoons egg whites (7 to 8 large egg whites)
    5½ cups (1 pound) unsweetened, dried, and shredded coconut
    the butter and sugar mixture

Place the electric mixer bowl over a water bath and heat until the mixture is hot to the touch. Attach the bowl to the electric mixer and, with a paddle attachment, mix on low until cool.

Place the macaroon mixture into a pastry bag fitted with a coupler. Pipe 1-inch dollops onto the cookie sheets 1 inch apart. Bake for 3 to 5 minutes, or until golden brown on the edges. Let the cookies cool in the pans for 5 minutes, then transfer the cookies to a wire rack to cool completely.

Melt:

    2 cups dark wafer chocolate or 12 ounces semisweet chocolate (tempered; see page 19)

Dip the bottom half of each macaroon in the chocolate and set it to dry on a cookie sheet lined with parchment paper.

almond fingers

Cozy up to a roaring fire with a mug of hot cocoa and some of these light, crispy, and elegant finger cookies. Sometimes known as Cat's Tongues (*langues de chat* in French), they are sprinkled with sliced almonds and sandwiched with melted chocolate after baking.

Preheat the oven to 350°F.

Line 2 cookie sheets with parchment paper.

Set aside:

1½ pounds (7 cups) sliced natural almonds

In a large bowl of an electric mixer at medium speed, cream:

8 ounces (2 sticks) unsalted butter, softened

1 cup sugar

Gradually mix in the following, adding more egg whites only after the last addition has been fully incorporated:

1 cup egg whites (6 to 7 egg whites)

1 teaspoon vanilla extract

Continue mixing at medium speed until well creamed.

Add and mix at low speed until combined:

1⅔ cups all-purpose flour

Gently scoop the dough into a pastry bag with a #12 round tip (or cut a small hole in a new pastry bag and use no tip). Pipe 3-inch lines of dough 1 inch apart on the cookie sheets.

Cover one pan of cookies generously with the sliced almonds. Holding the two back corners of the parchment paper and the pan, lift the pan and shake off the excess almonds onto a piece of parchment paper. Repeat with the second pan. Save the leftover almonds for a snack—maybe lightly toasting them.

Bake the cookies for 15 to 20 minutes, or until golden brown. Let the pans cool completely on a wire rack.

Melt:

12 ounces semisweet chocolate

Pour the melted chocolate into a pastry cone. Cut a medium tip on the end of the cone. Turn half of the cookies upside down. Pipe chocolate onto the overturned cookies and sandwich the flat sides of both cookies together.

As an alternative, place melted chocolate in a bowl. Dip the flat side of one cookie in the chocolate and sandwich with the flat side of another cookie. Repeat with the remaining cookies.

bar cookies

Bar cookies are incredibly satisfying. The combination of different flavors and textures in a single treat creates a delicious cacophony in your mouth. Some of these cookies can be a tad more time-consuming to make because they combine more than one recipe, but when you bite into one, we think you'll agree they are well worth the effort. Cut them into bite-size squares for a party, or cut them into larger 3 × 3-inch squares if you want to give them as Christmas gifts. They make a terrific alternative to the traditional Christmas butter cookies.

lemon crumble bars

We sell these tangy bars at the bakery year-round, but they make a perfect Christmas gift for a favorite teacher or mail carrier: Just cut the bars into 3-inch instead of 2-inch squares, wrap a few together in a large sheet of clear cellophane, and trim with a holiday bow. Lemon curd nestled in a shortbread crust and covered with a crumb topping gives off an opalescent shimmer. ▲▲▲

* * MAKES 1 DOZEN BARS * *

Preheat the oven to 350°F.

Lightly grease the bottom and sides of a cookie sheet. In addition, line the bottom of the pan with parchment paper.

In a large bowl of an electric mixer at medium speed, mix until well combined:

> 1 pound (4 sticks) unsalted butter, softened
> 1 cup sugar
> 1 tablespoon grated lemon zest

Add and mix at low speed, until just combined:

> 3½ cups all-purpose flour

Press the dough evenly into and up the sides of the cookie sheet. Bake for 15 to 18 minutes, or until pale golden brown. Let the cookies cool in the pans for 5 minutes, then transfer the cookies to a wire rack to cool completely.

In a large bowl of an electric mixer at low speed, combine:

> 6 ounces (1½ sticks) cold unsalted butter, cubed
> 1½ cups all-purpose flour
> ½ cup dark brown sugar, packed
> ¼ cup granulated sugar

Continue mixing at low speed until the mixture is crumbly and the butter is in pea-size bits. Set the crumb topping aside. Spread 2½ cups good-quality lemon curd evenly over the cooled crust. Sprinkle the crumb topping evenly over the curd. Bake for 10 to 15 minutes, or until the crumb topping is golden brown. Let cool in the pan. Cut into 2-inch squares.

christmas rainbow cookies

This marzipan "cake" is tinted red, white, and green, perfect for the Christmas season. It is layered with raspberry jam and covered in a thin layer of melted chocolate—so luscious! It remains one of the most requested cookies at our bakery. Be sure to start baking the day before you want to serve them. 🌲🌲🌲

Preheat the oven to 350°F.

Lightly grease the bottom and sides of 3 cookie sheets. In addition, line the bottom of each pan with parchment paper.

In a large bowl of an electric mixer with a paddle attachment, combine:

  2¼ cups sugar
    8 ounces (scant ¾ cup) almond paste, broken up
    1 large egg

Add and cream:

    1 pound (4 sticks) unsalted butter, softened
    1 teaspoon salt
  2½ teaspoons baking powder
    2 tablespoons milk powder
    1 tablespoon light corn syrup

Slowly add:

  1¾ cups eggs (7 to 8 eggs)

On a piece of wax paper, sift:

    4 cups cake flour

Add and mix at low speed until combined.

Add and mix until combined:

½ cup water

Divide the batter evenly into 3 bowls. Add approximately 4 drops of red food coloring to the first bowl. Add approximately 4 drops of green food coloring to the second bowl. Add more food coloring, drop by drop, if a darker color is desired. Leave the last bowl uncolored. Pour each of the batters onto a separate cookie sheet. Using a metal or plastic spatula, spread the batter evenly. Bake for 15 to 20 minutes, or until lightly colored on the edges or a skewer comes out clean. Let the cakes cool completely in their pans.

Stir until smooth:

⅔ cup raspberry jam

Run a bent spatula under the parchment paper of each baked cake to loosen them, leaving them in their pans. Evenly spread ⅓ cup of jam over the red layer. Take the white cake in its pan and flip the pan over the red layer. The cake should fall on top of the red; if necessary, ease it off with a spatula. Peel off the parchment paper and spread the remaining ⅓ cup of jam evenly on top.

Now flip the green cake on top of the white one, but do not remove the parchment paper. Place a pan, right side up, on top of the cake and carefully place a weight on top. Refrigerate the cake overnight.

Melt:

2 cups dark wafer chocolate or
12 ounces semisweet chocolate
(tempered; see page 19)

Remove the weight but not the top pan. Flip the pans over and, using a metal spatula or knife, ease the other pan off of the cake. Remove the paper from the red layer. Pour half of the chocolate on top of the assembled cake. Quickly spread the chocolate evenly in a thin layer over the entire top. If desired, drag a metal pastry comb over the top to create a lined pattern. Let the chocolate set for 10 minutes or until it is hard to the touch.

Gently place the other pan, right side up, on top of the cake and carefully flip the entire cake, holding firmly onto both pans. Remove the top pan, and the parchment paper from the green layer, and pour the remaining chocolate over the top. Spread and decorate as before. Let rest until set but not completely hardened. Using a paring knife dipped in hot water, cut the cake into 2-inch cubes. To maintain freshness, wrap in plastic wrap.

raspberry almond squares

Raspberry's ruby glow makes these bars a yuletide tradition at the Bakehouse. And any sweet treat that includes caramel is a favorite of mine. This rich, chewy, and buttery bar is layered with raspberry jam and caramelized almonds. Be careful: One is never enough. 🌲🌲🌲

* * MAKES 4 DOZEN SQUARES * *

Preheat the oven to 350°F.

Lightly grease the bottom and sides of a cookie sheet. In addition, line the bottom of the pan with parchment paper.

* CRUST:

In a large bowl of an electric mixer at medium speed, cream lightly:

1 pound (4 sticks) unsalted butter, softened
½ cup dark brown sugar, packed
½ cup granulated sugar

Add and mix at low speed until well combined:

3⅔ cups all-purpose flour

Press the dough evenly into and up the sides of the cookie sheet. Prick with a fork. Bake for 15 minutes, or until lightly browned. Let cool.

* FILLING:

In a small saucepan on low heat, melt:

9 ounces (2¼ sticks) unsalted butter

Add and mix until combined:

1¼ cups dark brown sugar, packed
⅔ cup light corn syrup
a pinch of salt

Whisk the mixture to combine well. Bring to a boil and boil for 3 minutes.

Remove from the heat and add:

10 ounces (2 cups) chopped natural almonds
10 ounces (3 cups) sliced almonds

* ASSEMBLY:

Stir until smooth:

⅓ cup raspberry jam

Spread the jam evenly over the cooled crust. Pour the almond mixture over the jam and spread evenly.

Bake for 20 to 25 minutes, or until the surface is bubbly and browned. Let cool completely in the pan. Run a paring knife around the edge of the crust to help it release from the pan. Place a board or another sheet pan of the same size as the cookie sheet on top and, holding onto both pans, turn them over. The raspberry bar should release easily from the pan. Now place the original pan, bottom to bottom, onto the raspberry bar and reverse again. Cut into 2-inch squares. To maintain freshness, wrap in plastic wrap.

apricot-chocolate triangles

Apricot jam lends a tangy flavor to this cookie's brown-sugar crust. Layers of chopped chocolate and crunchy pecans further enhance the taste. They look gorgeous with all three edges dipped in chocolate, but you can also simply dust them with confectioners' sugar. Either way, they're special enough to serve after Christmas dinner. 🎄 🎄 🎄

* * MAKES 8 DOZEN TRIANGLES * *

Preheat the oven to 350°F.

Lightly grease the bottom and sides of a cookie sheet. In addition, line the bottom of the pan with parchment paper.

✳ CRUST:

In a large bowl of an electric mixer at low speed, combine:
>   3 *cups all-purpose flour*
>   ³⁄₄ *cup dark brown sugar, packed*

Gradually add and mix at low speed until well combined:
>   12 *ounces (3 sticks) cold unsalted butter, cubed*
>   2 *teaspoons vanilla extract*

Press the dough evenly into the cookie sheet. Bake for 15 minutes, or until golden brown. Let the pan cool completely on a wire rack.

✳ FILLING:

In the bowl of an electric mixer at medium speed, whip to stiff peaks:
>   6 *large egg whites*

Mix together and fold into the egg whites:
>   6 *ounces (1½ cups) chopped pecans*
>   1½ *cups dark brown sugar, packed*

✳ ASSEMBLY:

Stir until smooth:
>   ³⁄₄ *cup apricot jam*

Spread the jam evenly over the cooled crust.

In a food processor, finely chop:
>   6 *ounces semisweet or bittersweet chocolate*

Sprinkle the chocolate over the jam.

Pour the pecan mixture over the jam and chocolate and spread evenly.

Bake for 20 to 25 minutes or until bubbly.
Let cool in the pan. Cut into 2-inch squares.
Cut each square diagonally in half.

Melt:

>   2 cups dark wafer chocolate or
>   12 ounces semisweet chocolate
>   (tempered; see page 19)

Dip the edges of each triangle in chocolate.
Let them set on parchment paper.

VARIATIONS * *As an alternative, substitute raspberry jam (or your favorite flavor) for the apricot jam, and dip the edges in melted white chocolate.*

• In addition, to add a touch of holiday pizzazz, before the chocolate sets, sprinkle the top with red and green nonpareils.

bethlehem brownies

At the bakery we commonly refer to these brownies as "death-defying brownies." I think that sums up just how rich they are—perfect for this festive time of year. These dense, scrumptious treats are topped with creamy coconut and chocolate chips. For the holidays, spruce them up by topping them with red and green M&M's or Sno-Caps. 🌲🌲🌲

** MAKES 4 DOZEN BROWNIES **

Preheat the oven to 350°F.

Lightly grease the sides and bottom of a 12 × 16 × 3-inch pan. In addition, line the bottom of the pan with parchment paper.

* BROWNIE:

In a large bowl of an electric mixer at medium speed, cream well:

 1   *pound (4 sticks) unsalted butter, softened*
 4   *cups granulated sugar*

Add and cream well:

 8   *large eggs*
 1   *tablespoon vanilla extract*

On a piece of wax paper, sift together:

 2   *cups all-purpose flour*
 3/4 *cup cocoa powder*
 1/2 *teaspoon salt*

Add to the butter mixture and mix at low speed, until combined.

Fold in:

 1 1/4 *cups (7 1/2 ounces) semisweet chocolate chips*
 1 1/2 *cups (6 ounces) chopped walnuts*

Spread evenly in the pan. Bake for 35 to 45 minutes, or until a skewer comes out with a few moist crumbs. Let the pan cool completely on a wire rack.

* TOPPING:

In a bowl of an electric mixer at medium speed, cream until light:

 12 *ounces (3 sticks) unsalted butter, softened*
 1 1/4 *cups dark brown sugar, packed*

Add and mix at low speed, until just combined:

> ³⁄₄ cup heavy cream
>
> 3 cups sweetened shredded coconut

Spread the coconut mixture evenly over the cooled brownie. Broil until the top is browned.

While still hot, sprinkle the top with:

> 1 cup chocolate chips, M&M's, or Sno-Caps

Refrigerate overnight. Cut into 2-inch squares to serve.

chocolate or walnut tartlets

This sweet tart dough, baked in miniature tart pans, can be filled with a rich and elegant chocolate ganache or a spicy Christmas walnut filling lightly flavored with cinnamon and cloves, depending on your whim. For a festive touch, you can gild the chocolate tartlets with edible gold dust. 🌲 🌲 🌲

✶ ✶ MAKES 4 DOZEN TARTLETS ✶ ✶

✱ DOUGH:

In a large bowl of an electric mixer at medium speed, cream:

> 8   *ounces (2 sticks) unsalted butter, softened*
> ⅓   *cup sugar*
> 1   *teaspoon vanilla extract*

Add and continue mixing:

> 1   *large egg*

Add and mix at low speed until well combined:

> 2½   *cups all-purpose flour*

Wrap the dough in plastic wrap and chill for at least 1 hour or overnight.

Preheat the oven to 350°F.

Grease forty-eight 1½-inch miniature tart shells or 4 mini muffin tins.

Form heaping teaspoonfuls of the dough into balls. Press each ball into the bottom and up the sides of the tart shells or mini muffin tins. The dough should be flush with the top of the shell and none of the shell should be exposed on the inside. Place the shells on a cookie sheet and chill.

If you are making the walnut tartlets, prepare the filling as the dough chills. If you are making the chocolate tartlets, bake the shells for 10 minutes, or until golden, and cool them as you prepare the ganache filling.

In a small saucepan, combine:

    5 ounces (1½ cups) medium-fine-
    chopped walnuts

    ⅔ cup sugar

    ⅔ cup milk or heavy cream

    2 tablespoons rum

    ¼ teaspoon ground cinnamon
    pinch of ground cloves
    pinch of ground nutmeg

Cook over low heat until the sugar dissolves. Increase the heat to medium and simmer until slightly thickened, about 7 minutes. Let cool. Pour the filling to the top of each tart shell. Bake for 15 to 18 minutes, or until browned.

Over a double boiler, melt:

    8 ounces semisweet chocolate, coarsely
    chopped

In a small saucepan, heat to a simmer, being careful not to burn:

    1 cup heavy cream

In the bowl of an electric mixer with a whisk attachment, whip the melted chocolate and scalded cream at low speed for 10 minutes, or until cooled slightly.

If you desire, stir in:

    2 tablespoons Grand Marnier

Pour the ganache to the top of each prebaked and cooled tart shell. Chill in the refrigerator for 1 hour, or until the ganache has set.

christmas cutout cookies

Time to get out the cookie cutters that have been hidden away in your drawer all year because holiday cookie cutters are a sure way to make any cookie Christmassy. And don't forget to keep an eye out for new and fun cookie cutters wherever you go. Maybe that bear cookie cutter you found can become the perfect Christmas teddy bear, with its own bright red bow. Our holiday cookie-cutter collection includes Rudolphs, Santas, trees, snowmen, stars, bells, and more. And remember, if you don't have the design you want, you can cut out a template from cardboard.

shortbread snowflakes

The beauty of these cookies, glistening with white sanding sugar like freshly fallen snow, lies in their simplicity. We can't make enough of them at Christmas. And I can understand why—I've always loved shortbread cookies. Could it be their amazing butteriness? 🌲🌲

** MAKES 4 TO 5 DOZEN COOKIES **

Preheat the oven to 350°F.

Grease 2 cookie sheets.

On a piece of wax paper, sift together:

    4   cups all-purpose flour
    1   cup confectioners' sugar
    ¼   teaspoon salt

Place the flour mixture into a large bowl of an electric mixer.

Add and mix on low until the dough comes together:

    1   pound (4 sticks) cold butter, cut into
        ½-inch cubes

On a lightly floured board, roll the dough out to a thickness of ¼ to 3/8 inch. Cut out with snowflake cookie cutters. Arrange 1 inch apart on the cookie sheets. Prick each cookie with a fork. Sprinkle lightly with white sanding sugar. Bake for 10 to 15 minutes, or until lightly colored. Let the cookies cool in the pans for 5 minutes, then transfer the cookies to a wire rack to cool completely.

rudolph chocolate shortbread

This recipe is a chocolate variation of our regular shortbread. We pipe a red chocolate nose on Rudolph and sprinkle it with red sanding sugar—see how it glows! 🌲🌲

Preheat the oven to 350°F.

Grease 2 cookie sheets.

On a piece of wax paper, sift together:

$3^{1}/_{2}$ *cups all-purpose flour*

$^{1}/_{2}$ *cup cocoa powder*

1 *cup confectioners' sugar*

$^{1}/_{4}$ *teaspoon salt*

Place the ingredients in a large bowl of an electric mixer.

Add:

17 *ounces (4 sticks plus 2 tablespoons) cold unsalted butter, cut into $^{1}/_{2}$-inch cubes*

Mix on low speed until the dough comes together.

On a lightly floured board, roll out the dough ¼ inch thick. Use a Rudolph cookie cutter, or a cookie cutter of your choice, to cut out the dough. Place Rudolphs 2 inches apart on the cookie sheets. Prick each cookie once with a fork. Bake for 10 to 12 minutes. Let the cookies cool in the pans for 5 minutes, then transfer the cookies to a wire rack to cool completely. Do not attempt to move the cookies before they have completely cooled or the legs might break off.

Melt:

$^{1}/_{4}$ *cup white wafer chocolate or 2 ounces white chocolate*

Add to the melted chocolate and stir until well combined:

6 *drops of red candy color (add more or less as desired)*

Pour the melted chocolate into a pastry cone. Cut a small tip off the end of the cone. Pipe a red nose on each Rudolph.

Before the chocolate dries, sprinkle the noses with:

red sanding sugar

cream-cheese pastry crescents

These festive crescents, more like individual desserts than just cookies, are a perfect after-dinner treat to take to a holiday party. The cream-cheese pastry is filled with chopped nuts, raspberry jam, and cinnamon sugar. The raspberry-red of the jam bubbles to the edges, giving the cookie a Christmas glow. Some other cream-cheese doughs can be difficult to work with, but not this one. It's a dream, and you can use your imagination to change the fillings to your taste. We also make ours with chocolate, apricot jam, or currants. ✴ ✴ ✴

✴ ✴ MAKES 1 DOZEN COOKIES ✴ ✴

In a large bowl of an electric mixer at medium speed, cream:

> 6 ounces (1½ sticks) unsalted butter, softened
> 6 ounces cream cheese, softened

Add and mix at low speed until just combined:

> 1½ cups all-purpose flour

Divide the dough into 4 equal portions. On a lightly floured board, shape each portion into a ball and flatten into a 4-inch disk. Wrap the disks in plastic and chill them for at least 1 hour or overnight.

Preheat the oven to 350°F.

Grease 2 cookie sheets.

Stir until smooth:

> 1 cup raspberry jam

Finely chop and set aside:

> 2 ounces (½ cup) walnuts or pecans

In a small bowl, mix:

> 1 cup sugar
> 1 tablespoon cinnamon

On a lightly floured board, roll each disk into a 9-inch round. Spread a thin coat of raspberry jam evenly on each round. Sprinkle with nuts and cinnamon sugar. Cut into 12 wedges. Roll each wedge up starting with the wide end. Arrange the rolls 2 inches apart on the cookie sheets. Curl each roll into a crescent. Bake for 10 to 12 minutes, or until golden brown. Let the cookies cool in the pans for 5 minutes, then transfer the cookies to a wire rack to cool completely.

linzer stars and trees

This delicate cinnamon-almond cookie is sandwiched with raspberry jam and dusted with confectioners' sugar. At the Bakehouse, we like to cut them out in festive holiday shapes such as stars and trees. ❧ ❧ ❧

* * MAKES 4 TO 6 DOZEN COOKIES,
DEPENDING ON THE SIZE OF YOUR COOKIE CUTTERS * *

In a large bowl of an electric mixer at medium speed, cream:

> 4   sticks (1 pound) unsalted butter, softened
> 1   cup sugar

Add and mix at low speed until well combined:

> 4   cups all-purpose flour
> 5½   ounces (1 cup) ground almonds
> 1½   teaspoons ground cinnamon

Chill the dough for 30 minutes.

Preheat the oven to 350°F.

Grease 2 cookie sheets.

On a lightly floured board, roll the dough out ¼ inch thick. Cut out shapes using star and/or tree cookie cutters. Arrange ½ inch apart on the cookie sheets. Using a #6 round pastry tip, randomly cut small holes out of half of the trees. Using a miniature star cookie cutter, cut out a star from the middle of half of the star cookies. Bake the cookies for 10 to 12 minutes, or until golden brown.

Let the cookies cool in the pans for 5 minutes, then transfer the cookies to a wire rack to cool completely.

Stir until smooth:

> 1   cup raspberry jam, or jam of your choice

Place the jam in a pastry bag with a small round tip. Turn over the cookies without holes. Cover them with raspberry jam. Dust the remaining cookies (the ones with the cutouts) with confectioners' sugar. Carefully sandwich the tops and jam-covered bottoms together.

gianduja bells

Christmas bells are ringing! These delicious hazelnut cookies are rolled out and cut into bell shapes, then sandwiched with Nutella, which is a type of "gianduja," or nut-flavored chocolate. ✳✳✳

Preheat the oven to 350°F.

Line 2 cookie sheets with parchment paper.

On a sheet pan, toast for 8 to 10 minutes or until fragrant:

    4 ounces (1 cup) hazelnuts

When cool, finely chop the nuts, and set aside.

In a large bowl of an electric mixer, combine the chopped nuts with:

    1 cup sugar
    3 cups all-purpose flour

Add and mix at low speed until the dough comes together:

    12 ounces (3 sticks) cold unsalted
      butter, cut into ½-inch cubes

On a lightly floured board, roll the dough out ¼ inch thick. Cut out shapes using bell cookie cutters. Arrange 1 inch apart on the cookie sheets. Bake for 10 to 15 minutes, or until lightly colored. Let the pan cool completely on a wire rack.

Turn over half of the cookies. Place 1½ cups Nutella in a pastry bag with a small round tip. Pipe about 1 teaspoon of Nutella onto each of the turned cookies. Sandwich them together with the unturned cookies, bottom to bottom.

fancy decorated cookies

If you love to dress up your cookies with beautiful decorations, and if you are thrilled by a bit of a baking challenge, this is the chapter for you. Here, you'll find decorating ideas that range from the very simple to the complex, and projects that include simple iced cookies and complex three-dimensional Christmas tree creations. All of these cookies will be truly breathtaking, and if taken step by step, even the most advanced cookies can be made. Many of the recipes in this chapter make use of special ways to tint and shape chocolate. These fun decorative touches will make your cookies completely unique (and gorgeous).

COLORFUL CHOCOLATE
DESIGN TECHNIQUE

The recipes in the first section of this chapter use this simple and unique technique to make eye-catching chocolate designs. When they are used to top a big showstopping cookie, the effect is truly magnificent.

This method will show you how to make everything from the basic one-color polka dots and stars for the Christmas Tree (page 69) to the fancier Christmas Ornament Cookie (page 72), with several different colors and piping. Templates for the chocolate designs can be found at the back of the book (and any template can be enlarged or reduced on a photocopier to fit the scale of your cookie). Just remember to have fun; after all, you're painting with chocolate!

WHAT YOU WILL NEED:

Sheet pan
Parchment paper
Dark and/or white wafer chocolate
(see recipe for specific amount)
Candy colors (see recipe for recommended colors)
Pastry cones (see recipe for specific number)
Plus any Fun Extras called for in the recipe

HOW TO.

Photocopy or trace the template you will be using, or draw your own with a black marker. This will go beneath the parchment paper on which you pipe the chocolate to provide a guideline.

2. Place the template on a sheet pan or flat surface. Lay a sheet of parchment paper on top. Lightly secure the parchment paper with one or two pieces of tape.

3. Melt the chocolate (if you are using both white and dark chocolate, melt them separately). Divide the chocolate as indicated in the recipe you are using, and tint the portions with any specified candy colors until they achieve the desired colors. Pour the chocolate into one or more pastry cones.

4. Cut a hole in the pastry cone you will be using first, and keep the others warm on a barely simmering double boiler or remelt in the microwave as needed.

5. Trace the outline of the template with dark chocolate and fill in as indicated. Set aside to harden.

6. When it is dry, gently flip the design and carefully peel off the parchment paper.

7. If you'd like, dust the design with luster dust, or pipe on any additional decorations as indicated in the recipe.

christmas tree

It's time to trim the tree, only this tree is completely edible, from the trunk to the orna-ments! That American classic, the chocolate chip cookie, is decked out in true holiday spirit, baked in a Christmas-tree cake mold. Decorate it with green and yellow tinted chocolate and colored chocolate polka dots and stars. Fun to make and a sweet treat to eat, this tree makes a perfect gift or decoration for your holiday party. Make this cookie the day, or the day before, you plan on serving it. 🌲🌲🌲 for decorated cookie

WHAT YOU WILL NEED:

cookie:

1 Chocolate Chip Cookie Tree (page 71)

tools:

4 pastry cones

decoration:

3 cups white wafer chocolate to make branches, lights,
polka-dot ornaments, and a star

colors:

green, yellow, red, and blue candy colors

HOW TO:

1. Bake the cookie and let it cool completely.

2. Melt the white chocolate. Pour ½ cup of the melted white chocolate into a bowl and tint it green. Divide the remaining melted chocolate among 3 bowls. Tint the chocolate in each bowl a different color: yellow, red, and blue. Pour the colored chocolates into separate pastry bags. Cut medium-size holes in the yellow, red, and blue pastry bags.

3. On a sheet pan lined with parchment paper, pipe out colored polka dots in red and blue. Pipe out a large star in yellow. Set aside to harden.

4. Place the cookie on a sturdy and flat serving plate or base. Cut a medium-size hole in the green pastry cone and pipe out branches onto your cake. As a simple alternative, cut a large hole in the green bag and drizzle the chocolate over the tree cookie.

5. Diagonally pipe small yellow dots in lines randomly on the tree so that they resemble Christmas lights.

6. Adhere the polka dots to the cookie with dabs of chocolate. Do the same for the star that adorns the top of the tree.

CHOCOLATE CHIP COOKIE TREE

Everyone loves chocolate chip cookies year-round, but for the holidays, why not try something a little different and bake the dough in a tree-shaped cake pan? These special pans are available at many cookware and baking supply stores. Any extra dough should be immediately spooned onto a cookie sheet and baked for yourself as a reward for all of your hard work. Alternatively, the dough can be portion-wrapped and frozen so you will always be ready to bake cookies for unexpected guests.

** MAKES 1 LARGE COOKIE OR 4 DOZEN INDIVIDUAL COOKIES **

Preheat the oven to 350°F.

Grease and flour a 2-inch deep tree-shaped cake pan (ours was 15 inches long and used 5¹/₂ cups of batter).

Or, if you're baking individual cookies, grease two cookie sheets.

In a large bowl of an electric mixer at medium speed, cream:

> 1 *pound (4 sticks) unsalted butter, softened*
> 1¹/₂ *cups granulated sugar*
> 1¹/₄ *cups dark brown sugar, packed*

Add and cream:

> 4 *large eggs*
> 1¹/₂ *teaspoons vanilla extract*

In a separate bowl, mix together:

> 4¹/₂ *cups all-purpose flour*
> 2 *teaspoons baking soda*
> ¹/₂ *teaspoon salt*

Add to the butter mixture and mix at low speed until a soft dough forms.

Stir in:

> 3 *cups semisweet chocolate chips*

Place 5¹/₂ cups of the dough into the pan (adjust the amount as needed for your pan's dimensions) and spread evenly. Bake for 28 to 35 minutes, or until a skewer inserted in the center of the cookie comes out clean. (Bake individual cookies for 8 to 10 minutes.) Let the pan cool for 30 minutes on a wire rack and then turn out the cookie onto a wire rack or serving plate. Let cool completely.

christmas ornament cookie

As a child, I loved the glistening glass blown ornaments on our tree most of all. Even when they became old and the mirroring began to crack or discolor, I thought they were beautiful; they sparkled brilliantly as they reflected the many colors of the Christmas lights. Although not quite as glittering, this edible ornament is sure to be a stunner. A delicious peanut butter cookie is baked in round cake pans and decorated with tinted white chocolate. The ornament hanger is made of solid gilded chocolate. To simplify the design, just decrease the number of colors and pipe fewer details on the ornament. 🎄🎄🎄 for decorated cookie

WHAT YOU WILL NEED:

cookie:

one 9-inch round Peanut Butter Cookie (page 74)

tools:

6 pastry cones

decoration:

2 cups white wafer chocolate and 1¹/₂ cups dark wafer chocolate to make ornament hanger and ornament decoration

colors:

red, green, yellow, royal blue, and sky blue candy colors

fun extras:

gold or silver luster dust, and dragées

HOW TO:

1. Bake the cookie and let it cool completely.

2. Melt the white and dark chocolates separately. Divide the melted white chocolate among 5 bowls. Tint the chocolate blue, red, yellow, and green, keeping the remaining bowl of white chocolate uncolored. Pour the dark chocolate and colored chocolates into separate pastry cones.

3. Using the template provided on page 92, pipe out the ornament hanger in dark chocolate using the method on page 67. When the decoration has hardened, use a paintbrush to lightly dust it with gold luster dust.

4. Place the cookie on a sturdy, flat serving plate or base.

5. Cut small holes in the pastry cones and pipe decorations of your choosing on the ornament freehand.

6. Adhere the ornament hanger to the top with a large dot of melted chocolate; gently hold it in place until the chocolate begins to set.

NOTE *A quick alternative to the ornament design is to drizzle tinted chocolate, Jackson Pollock–style, over the top of the cookie. Go crazy—the more colors the merrier.*

PEANUT BUTTER COOKIE

Not only is this recipe delicious on its own, but also try sandwiching individual cookies together with raspberry jam for a PB&J treat that Santa, and your kids, will love.

Preheat the oven to 350°F.

Grease and flour two 9-inch cake pans (2 inches deep). Line the pans with parchment paper cut into 9-inch circles. Or, if baking individual cookies, grease 2 cookie sheets.

In a large bowl of an electric mixer at medium speed, cream:

  8 ounces (2 sticks) unsalted butter, softened
  1 cup granulated sugar
  1 cup dark brown sugar, packed
  1 cup chunky peanut butter
  1 teaspoon vanilla extract

Add and thoroughly blend in:

  2 large eggs

In a separate bowl, mix together:

  $3^{1}/_{2}$ cups all-purpose flour
  2 teaspoons baking soda
  $^{1}/_{4}$ teaspoon salt

Add to the butter mixture and mix at low speed until a soft dough forms.

Divide the dough evenly between the 2 pans. Pat the dough down evenly. Bake for 35 to 40 minutes, or until a skewer inserted in the center of each cookie comes out clean. (Bake individual cookies for 8 to 10 minutes.) Let the pan cool for 20 minutes on a wire rack. Turn each cookie out onto a plate, remove the parchment paper, and turn right side up. Let cool completely.

celestial wreath

Wreaths are a welcoming decoration on a front door—not just for Christmas, but for the entire winter season. This cookie is baked in a ring-shaped cake pan. Decorate it with chocolate moon, star, and sun ornaments in honor of the winter solstice, and top it off with a chocolate bow. The background is simply drizzled chocolate and sprinkled dragées.

🌲🌲🌲 for decorated cookie

WHAT YOU WILL NEED:

cookie:

one 9-inch ring of Oatmeal Raisin Cookie (page 77)

tools:

6 pastry cones

decoration:

3 cups white wafer chocolate to make celestial ornaments

colors:

royal blue, sky blue, yellow, and orange candy colors

fun extras:

gold and/or silver luster dust, dragées

HOW TO:

1. Bake the cookie and let it cool completely.

2. Melt the white chocolate and divide between 2 bowls. Tint the chocolate in one bowl pale blue and pour one-third of it into a large pastry cone. Tint the leftover chocolate in the bowl a darker blue and pour half of it into a pastry cone. Finally, tint the remaining chocolate in the bowl midnight blue and pour it into a third pastry cone. Tint the second bowl of chocolate light yellow, pour one-third of it into a pastry cone and tint the leftover a darker yellow, and pour half of the darker yellow into another pastry cone. Finally, tint the remaining chocolate orange and pour it into a third pastry cone.

3. Using the templates provided on page 92, pipe out celestial ornaments using the method on page 67. When the decorations have hardened, flip them over and use a paintbrush to lightly dust them with luster dusts. Set the celestial ornaments aside.

4. Drizzle the leftover chocolate in the pastry cones over the ring. Sprinkle some dragées on top before the chocolate has set.

5. Place the cookie on a sturdy, flat serving plate or base.

6. Adhere the celestial ornaments to the top with dots of melted chocolate.

OATMEAL RAISIN COOKIE

Another of Liv's all-time favorite cookies, our oatmeal raisin has a cinnamony accent perfect for the holidays and yummy enough for any time of year. It is not overly sweet, so it is a nice alternative to the indulgent chocolate chip variety. 🌲 for undecorated cookies

** MAKES 1 LARGE COOKIE OR 2 DOZEN INDIVIDUAL COOKIES **

Preheat the oven to 350°F.

Grease and flour a 9-inch ring-shaped cake pan with a 2-inch hole. Or, if baking individual cookies, grease a cookie sheet.

In a large bowl of an electric mixer at medium speed, cream:

    5 ounces (1 stick plus 2 tablespoons) unsalted butter, softened
    3/4 cup granulated sugar
    1/3 cup dark brown sugar, packed

Add and thoroughly incorporate:

    1 large egg
    1/2 teaspoon vanilla extract

On a piece of wax paper, sift together:

    3 3/4 cups all-purpose flour
    2 1/4 teaspoons baking soda
    1/2 teaspoon cinnamon
    1/2 teaspoon salt

Add and mix at low speed, until a soft dough forms.

Add and mix until incorporated:

    1 cup rolled oats

Stir in:

    3/4 cup raisins

Pat the dough evenly into the pan. Bake for 35 to 40 minutes, or until a skewer inserted in the middle of the cookie comes out clean. (Bake individual cookies for 8 to 10 minutes.) Let the pan cool for 20 minutes on a wire rack. Turn out the cookie onto a plate and let cool completely.

norwegian "knitted" cookies

In honor of my heritage, I like to make large cookies in the shape of mittens, hats, and sweaters decorated with royal icing, chocolate, and sanding sugar to resemble the clothing my Norwegian grandmother knitted for me. But these cookies can be cut out to resemble any motif you desire: snowmen, Christmas presents, nutcrackers, angels, teddy bears, ornaments, or Christmas trees. You can look for cookie cutters or design your own templates and cut them out of cardboard. Use these basic instructions as a guideline for any other decoration of your choice, and feel free to use the extra royal icing to decorate your other holiday cookies. ♣♣♣ for decorated cookies

WHAT YOU WILL NEED:

cookie:
Sugar Cookie dough (page 80)

tools:
cookie cutters or hand-made cardboard templates
5 pastry cones

decoration:
1 recipe Royal Icing (page 80) and 1 cup dark wafer chocolate for hat and accents

colors:
light blue, red, green, and yellow liquid gel colors,
or colors of your choice

fun extras:
white sanding sugar

1. Using the sweater image provided on page 92, cut out a cardboard template.

2. On a lightly floured surface, roll out the sugar cookie dough ¼ inch thick. Chill for 10 minutes. Place the template on the dough. Cut out the sweater by running a paring knife around the edge of the template. Carefully slide a metal spatula under the cookie and transfer it to a greased cookie sheet. Use any excess dough to cut out mittens and hats, or any other holiday motifs of your choice. Arrange the cookies 1 inch apart on the cookie sheet.

3. Bake the cookies according to the recipe and let them cool completely.

4. Reserve 1½ cups of royal icing. Divide the remaining royal icing equally among 4 bowls. Tint the icing light blue, red, green, and yellow. Keep the bowls covered with a damp cloth. Place the colored icings in separate pastry cones. Cut small holes in each.

5. Melt the dark chocolate. Pour the chocolate into a pastry cone. Keep the chocolate warm on a barely simmering double boiler or remelt in the microwave as needed.

6. Spread a thin layer of white royal icing over the entire cookie. Immediately pour white sanding sugar over the top. Shake or dust off any excess sugar.

7. Using the photo below as a guideline, pipe out the upside-down-V pattern, the outline, any details, and the collar in dark chocolate.

8. When the chocolate has set, following the template for guidance if necessary, pipe out the collar pattern with the colored royal icings. Let dry completely overnight.

NOTE *A quick alternative to decorating with royal icing is to stick chocolate chips, nonmelting candies, or sprinkles on the cut-out cookies before baking.*

SUGAR COOKIES

This basic sugar cookie dough is strong enough to be cut into large and small cookies alike, and the cookies are durable enough to stand up to a lot of decorating. ♣♣ for cutout cookies

Preheat the oven to 350°F.

Grease 2 cookie sheets.

In the bowl of an electric mixer at medium speed, cream:

    8 ounces (2 sticks) unsalted butter, softened

    1⅓ cups sugar

Add and thoroughly incorporate:

    2 large eggs

    ½ teaspoon vanilla extract

On a piece of wax paper, sift together:

    3¾ cups all-purpose flour

    1 tablespoon baking powder

    1 teaspoon salt

On a lightly floured board, roll the dough out ¼ inch thick. Cut out shapes with cookie cutters, or using cardboard templates as a guide. Arrange the cookies 1 inch apart on the cookie sheets. Bake for 10 to 15 minutes, or until lightly colored. Let the cookies cool in the pans for 5 minutes, then transfer the cookies to a wire rack to cool completely.

ROYAL ICING

In a large bowl of a clean electric mixer fitted with a whip attachment, whip to stiff peaks:

    ¼ cup plus 1 tablespoon meringue powder

    ½ cup cold water

Add and mix at low speed with a paddle attachment, until combined:

    4½ cups (1 pound 5 ounces) confectioners' sugar

Continue mixing at high speed for 5 to 8 minutes, or until the icing is stiff.

Add and mix on low speed until combined:

    ½ teaspoon strained fresh lemon juice

Cover the bowl with a damp cloth while you are working with or coloring the icing, or immediately place it in an airtight container or pastry cone; otherwise, a hard crust will quickly form as it dries.

gingerbread fireplace

What would Christmas be without spicy, festive gingerbread? Here's an amazing new gingerbread project we know you'll love (the more traditional gingerbread house follows). You can assemble the gingerbread house or fireplace one day and decorate it the next, or condense the work into one day; just be a bit more careful when making it all in one day because the structure will not have set completely. 🌲🌲🌲 for three-dimensional cookies

WHAT YOU WILL NEED:

cookie:

Gingerbread Cookie dough (page 87)

tools:

*pastry bag with a # 8 round tip and
15 pastry cones*

decoration:

*1 recipe Royal Icing (at left), 2 cups white wafer chocolate, and
3 cups dark wafer chocolate to make mantel, stockings, candles, plate
of cookies, Santa's note, fireplace utensils, and braided rug*

colors:

red liquid gel and blue, green, yellow, red, and pink candy colors

fun extras:

red sanding sugar, 3 to 5 Tootsie Rolls, red and green M&M's

HOW TO:

1. Preheat the oven to 350°F. Line 3 cookie sheets with parchment paper.

2. Cut out the cardboard templates using the templates provided on page 93.

3. On a lightly floured surface, roll out the gingerbread dough ¼ inch thick. Place the cardboard templates on the dough and run a paring knife around

the edge of each. You will need 1 front, 1 back, 2 sides, and 1 bottom of the fireplace. In addition cut out the smaller inner hearth cookies: 2 sides, the back, and the top. Carefully slide a metal spatula under each cookie and transfer it to a cookie sheet. Arrange the cookies 1 inch apart.

4. Bake the cookies for 12 to 15 minutes, or until lightly browned on the edges, and let them cool completely.

5. Using the templates provided, make as many of the chocolate accessories as you'd like (3 stockings, Santa's note, the plate of cookies, fireplace utensils, candles, candy cane, teddy bear, and the braided rug) using the method on page 67.

6. Using the template provided, pipe out the chocolate mantel, at least $\frac{1}{8}$ to $\frac{1}{4}$ inch thick.

7. Place 1 cup of royal icing in a small bowl and tint it red. Place another 2 cups in another bowl and leave it white. Split the remaining icing into 3 bowls and tint it green, orange, and yellow. Keep the bowls covered with a damp cloth as you work. Place the green, yellow, and orange icings in separate pastry cones. Fill another pastry cone with red, reserving the remainder. Fill yet another pastry cone with white royal icing and place the remaining white icing into a pastry bag with a coupler and a #8 round tip. Cut small- to medium-size holes in all of the pastry cones.

8. With a small offset spatula, spread a thin layer of the remaining red royal icing over the fireplace cookies. Immediately sprinkle red sanding sugar over the top. Shake or dust off any excess sugar.

9. Using the white pastry cone, pipe out the mortar lines between the bricks.

10. Assemble the fireplace using the white royal icing in the pastry bag with the #8 tip. Adhere the fireplace base to a flat plate or a sturdy base with a dab of royal icing. Pipe more white royal icing around the base's circumference and adhere the back to the longest side. Pipe icing up both side edges of the back. Firmly adhere the sides to the base and back. Assemble the hearth interior in the same manner with royal icing and attach it with royal icing

to the base. Lastly, pipe white royal icing on all remaining exposed edges. Attach the front of the fireplace. Make sure every side is securely in place and as level as possible. Pipe icing around the top edge and place the chocolate mantel on top.

11. Pipe royal icing up each edge of the fireplace and stick red M&M's or a small candy of your choice to the edges.

12. Using the colored royal icings, pipe red, orange, and yellow flames in the hearth.

13. Pipe green fir branches on top of the mantel, mounding them up in the center to give some height. Stick the chocolate candles into the greenery.

14. Adhere the stockings to the mantel edge with melted chocolate, gently holding them in place until the chocolate has set. Pipe white royal icing fur over the stockings. Adhere the candy cane to one stocking and the teddy bear to another.

15. Adhere the plate of cookies and Santa's note to the mantel with a dab of chocolate.

16. Adhere the utensils and the hearth cover to the fireplace with dabs of icing. Lastly, adhere the rug in front of the fireplace with a dab of icing.

17. Let dry completely overnight.

gingerbread house

WHAT YOU WILL NEED:

cookie:

Gingerbread Cookie dough (page 87)

tools:

pastry bag with a coupler, a #8 round tip, and a #5 round tip

decoration:

1 recipe Royal Icing (page 80) made very stiff with additional confectioners' sugar

fun extras:

white sanding sugar, chopped Life Savers candy for windows, and assorted Christmas candy including gum drops, M&M's, and candy canes (dragées and white nonpareils are optional)

HOW TO MAKE A GINGERBREAD HOUSE:

1. Preheat the oven to 350°F. Line 3 cookie sheets with parchment paper.

2. Cut out cardboard templates using the templates provided on page 94.

3. On a lightly floured surface, roll out the gingerbread dough ¼ inch thick. Place the cardboard templates on the dough and run a paring knife around the edge of each template. You will need 1 front, 1 back, 2 sides, 1 bottom, 2 roof panels, and 3 chimney pieces. Carefully slide a metal spatula under each cookie and transfer it to a cookie sheet. Arrange the cookies 1 inch apart. Cut windows out of the two sides and the back of the house.

4. Bake the cookies for 5 minutes, then carefully pour the broken Life Savers into the window holes. Continue baking for 8 to 10 minutes, or until the candy is melted and the edges of the cookies are lightly browned. Let them cool completely.

5. Spread a thin layer of royal icing onto the two roof panels and sprinkle them with white sanding sugar, and with nonpareils and dragées if you like, to give the effect of snow.

6. Place the remaining royal icing into the pastry bag with a coupler and the #8 round tip.

7. Adhere the bottom of the house to a flat, sturdy base or plate. Pipe royal icing around the perimeter of the base. Adhere the front of the house to one side of the base. Pipe royal icing up both side edges of the front. Adhere the sides to the front and the base and again pipe royal icing on the exposed edges of the sides. Adhere the back in the same manner.

8. Pipe royal icing around the top edges of the sides, front, and back. Place the roof panels evenly on top, adhering them to each other with more royal icing.

9. Pipe some royal icing in the center of the roof. Stick the chimney to this, adhering the three segments together with more icing.

10. Pipe a brick pattern around the chimney, covering the entire surface.

11. Pipe icing (one side at a time so the icing doesn't dry too fast) up the sides of the house. Stick M&M's or other small candies onto the icing. Do the same for the base of the house, but use larger, heavier candies. Stick gum drops to the top of the roof and light candies such as large Sno-Caps or chocolate-dipped pretzels to the roof edges.

12. Switch to a #5 tip and pipe the window trim. Pipe icicles hanging from the roof by lightly touching the roof with the tip, squeezing the bag, and releasing the pressure as you pull down.

13. Let dry completely overnight.

GINGERBREAD COOKIES

What would Christmas be without this traditional cookie? No gingerbread men and women for children to bite the arms off of, no gingerbread house to spice up your holiday decorations—it just wouldn't be the same. So here is our recipe. We hope you will make it every year.

* * MAKES 1 GINGERBREAD HOUSE,
1 GINGERBREAD FIREPLACE PLUS GINGERBREAD MEN AND WOMEN,
OR 2 DOZEN GINGERBREAD MEN AND WOMEN * *

Preheat the oven to 350°F.

Grease 3 cookie sheets.

In the bowl of an electric mixer at medium speed, cream until fluffy:

    8 ounces (2 sticks) unsalted butter, softened

    1 cup sugar

Add and mix until smooth:

    2 large eggs

    1/2 cup molasses

On a piece of wax paper, sift together:

    4 cups all-purpose flour

    2 tablespoons cocoa powder

    1/4 teaspoon salt

    1 3/4 tablespoons ground ginger

    1 tablespoon ground cinnamon

    2 teaspoons ground cloves

    1 teaspoon baking soda

Add to the butter mixture and mix at low speed until well combined.

Chill the dough for up to 8 hours or overnight.

On a lightly floured board, roll the dough out 1/4 inch thick. Cut out gingerbread men and women using cookie cutters, or, if making a fireplace or house, follow the instructions on pages 81 and 84. Arrange the cookies 1 inch apart on the cookie sheets. Bake for 10 to 12 minutes, or until lightly browned. Let the cookies cool in the pans for 5 minutes, then transfer the cookies to a wire rack to cool completely.

3-D christmas tree

We have to admit that this impressive cookie construction, though beautiful, is time-consuming. But the final result is so elegant that we couldn't resist including it in the book. This Christmas tree would make the perfect centerpiece for your holiday table. Of course, to simplify our design, you can cut out and stack concentric circles or stars instead of the complex snowflake shapes; this would save you an abundance of time. But for those of you who appreciate a vacation-time challenge, roll up your sleeves. 🌲🌲🌲

for decorated tree

WHAT YOU WILL NEED:

cookie:
Spice Cookie dough (page 90)

tools:
pastry bag with a coupler, a #4 round tip, and a #8 round tip

decoration:
*1 recipe Royal Icing (page 80),
2 tablespoons melted dark wafer chocolate to make 1 star*

fun extras:
silver and/or gold dragées, gold or silver luster dust

HOW TO:

1. Preheat the oven to 350°F. Line 3 cookie sheets with parchment paper.

2. Cut out cardboard templates using the templates provided on page 94.

3. On a lightly floured surface, roll out the spice cookie dough ¼ inch thick. Place the cardboard templates for snowflakes (or, if simplifying, circles or stars) on the dough and run a paring knife around the edge of each template. Cut out 2 of each size. You should end up with 22 snowflakes total. Carefully slide a metal spatula under each cookie and transfer it to a cookie sheet. Arrange the cookies 1 inch apart.

4. Bake the cookies for 10 to 12 minutes, or until golden brown, and let them cool completely.

5. Place the royal icing in the pastry bag with the coupler and the #8 tip. Adhere the largest cookie to a sturdy base or flat plate using a dab of royal icing. Pipe royal icing on top of the cookie, keeping the icing well within the 6 points of the snowflake.

6. Adhere the next cookie of the same size to the first, lining up the points of the snowflake in between the points of the first. Continue piping royal icing and stacking the cookies in the same manner, going in descending order of size until you have reached the smallest cookie.

7. Fill in empty areas between the cookies with royal icing; it will look like snow.

8. Change the pastry tip to the #4. Carefully pipe linear swags, starting and ending on the points of the snowflakes. Here's how: Holding the bag perpendicular to the cookie, lightly touch the point where you are to begin the swag with the tip of the pastry bag, and with consistent pressure, pipe a string from the top edge, down through the arch, then up to the top of the next snowflake point. Allow the icing to drape naturally in an arc as you squeeze the bag. Do not make the motion too slow or too fast or the swag will break before the arc is completed. Continue to create swags around the entire tree.

9. Pipe small dots of royal icing where the swags meet, and adhere dragées to these points.

10. Pour the melted chocolate into a pastry cone and cut a medium-size hole in its tip. Pipe a small star onto a sheet pan lined with parchment paper. Let set. When the chocolate is dry, dust both sides of the star with gold luster dust.

11. Pipe a dollop of royal icing on the top of the tree. Place one point of the star into the dollop.

12. Let dry completely overnight. The assembled tree can be stored at room temperature for 1 week. (Place the tree in a cardboard box of the same height, and wrap the box in plastic wrap.)

SPICE COOKIES

Each batch of cookies in the book had to be sampled by everyone on our staff, and this one was a surprise hit. No chocolate, no coconut, no caramel—just crisp and spicy. So, dust off your cookie cutters and let the smell of cinnamon and spice fill the air.

** MAKES 3 DOZEN REGULAR COOKIES, OR ENOUGH DOUGH TO CREATE
ONE 3-D CHRISTMAS TREE (PAGE 88) **

Preheat the oven to 350°F.

Grease 2 cookie sheets.

In a large bowl of an electric mixer at medium speed, cream:

 1 *pound (4 sticks) unsalted butter, softened*
 1 *cup granulated sugar*
 ¼ *cup dark brown sugar, packed*

Add and mix at medium speed:

 3 *egg yolks*
 ¼ *cup molasses*

On a piece of wax paper, sift together:

 4⅔ *cups all-purpose flour*
 2 *tablespoons ground cinnamon*
 2 *tablespoons ground ginger*
 1 *tablespoon ground cloves*
 ½ *teaspoon ground nutmeg*
 ¾ *teaspoon salt*

Add to the butter mixture and mix at low speed until well combined.

Chill the dough for 30 minutes.

On a lightly floured board, roll out the dough ¼ inch thick. Using a cookie cutter of your choice, cut out cookies and arrange them 1 inch apart on the cookie sheets. Bake for 8 to 10 minutes, or until browned. Let the cookies cool in the pans for 5 minutes, then transfer the cookies to a wire rack to cool completely.

TEMPLATES FOR CARDBOARD
COOKIE CUTTERS

To achieve the correct size for your cookies, each of the templates below and on pages 93 and 94 should be increased to four times their size, or by 400 percent on your photocopier.

CHRISTMAS ORNAMENT COOKIE

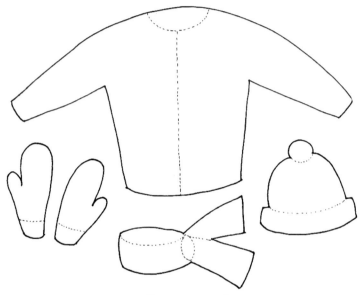

NORWEGIAN "KNITTED" COOKIES

CHRISTMAS TREE

CELESTIAL WREATH

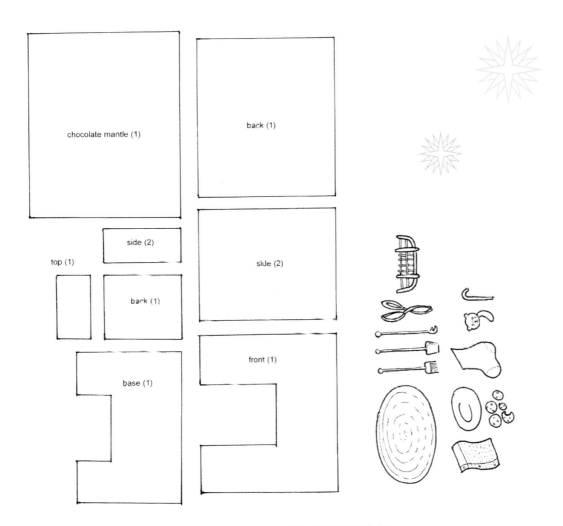

GINGERBREAD FIREPLACE

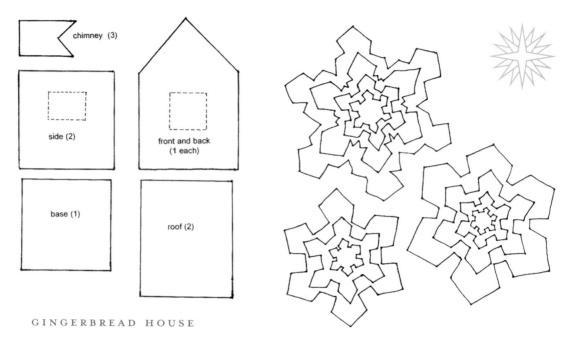

GINGERBREAD HOUSE

chimney (3)

side (2)

front and back
(1 each)

base (1)

roof (2)

3-D CHRISTMAS TREE

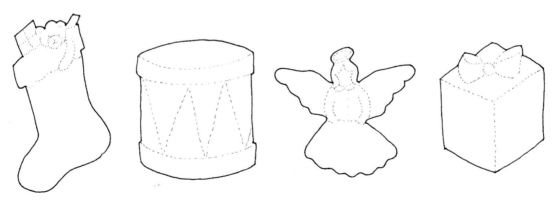

MORE CHRISTMAS COOKIES!

SUPPLIERS

The suppliers listed below stock baking and decorating tools and ingredients
that are not readily available in supermarkets.

THE FOODCRAFTER'S SUPPLY CATALOG
P.O. Box 442-OKD
Waukon, IA 52172-0442
800-776-0575
www.KitchenKrafts.com
A wide range of baking and decorating tools, from
cookie cutters to candymaking tools and ingredients.

KING ARTHUR FLOUR BAKER'S CATALOGUE
P.O. Box 876
Norwich, VT 05055-0876
800-827-6836
www.bakerscatalogue.com
Everything from springerle molds to sheet pans,
electric mixers to cookie presses, and flour to every
type of chocolate.

NEW YORK CAKE AND BAKING DISTRIBUTORS, INC.
56 West 22nd Street
New York, NY 10010
800-942-2539 or 212-675-7955
Decorating and baking supplies from food coloring
to pastry bags and tips.

WILLIAMS-SONOMA
Locations throughout the United States
877-812-6235
www.williams-sonoma.com
In addition to carrying most bakeware and many specialty baking ingredients, this national chain carries a
great array of Christmas cookie cutters and
decorating kits.

WILTON INDUSTRIES, INC.
2240 West 75th Street
Woodridge, IL 60517
800-794-5866
www.wilton.com
Decorating tools and ingredients, including wafer
chocolate, cookie cutters, and food colorings.

INDEX